D1011227

The
Losses
of
Our Lives

The Losses of Our Lives

The Sacred Gifts of Renewal in Everyday Loss

Dr. Nancy Copeland-Payton

Nancy Copeland-Payton

Walking Together, Finding the Way ®
SKYLIGHT PATHS®
PUBLISHING
Woodstock, Vermont

The Losses of Our Lives:
The Sacred Gifts of Renewal in Everyday Loss

2009 Hardcover Edition, First Printing
© 2009 by Nancy Copeland-Payton

All rights reserved. No part of this book may be reproduced or transmitted in any form or by any means, electronic or mechanical, including photocopying, recording, or by any information storage and retrieval system, without permission in writing from the publisher.

For information regarding permission to reprint material from this book, please mail or fax your request in writing to SkyLight Paths Publishing, Permissions Department, at the address / fax number listed below, or e-mail your request to permissions@skylightpaths.com.

Scripture quotations are from the *New Revised Standard Version Bible*, copyright 1989 by the Division of Christian Education of the National Council Churches of Christ in the USA. Used by permission. All rights reserved.

Grateful acknowledgment is given for permission to reprint the prayers by Sister Teresa Jackson, OSB, on pp. 12 and 131, © 2009 by Sister Teresa Jackson, OSB.

Library of Congress Cataloging-in-Publication Data
Copeland-Payton, Nancy.
  The losses of our lives : the sacred gifts of renewal in everyday loss / Nancy Copeland-Payton.
      p. cm.
  Includes bibliographical references.
  ISBN-13: 978-1-59473-271-3 (hardcover)
  ISBN-10: 1-59473-271-X (hardcover)
  1. Suffering—Religious aspects. 2. Loss (Psychology)—Religious aspects. 3. Spiritual life. 4. Spirituality. I. Title.
  BL65.S85C67 2009
  204'.42—dc22

                                                                    2009036406

10   9   8   7   6   5   4   3   2   1
Manufactured in the United States of America
Jacket Design: Tim Holtz
Jacket Art: ©iStockphoto.com/jcarroll-images modified by Tim Holtz

SkyLight Paths Publishing is creating a place where people of different spiritual traditions come together for challenge and inspiration, a place where we can help each other understand the mystery that lies at the heart of our existence.

SkyLight Paths sees both believers and seekers as a community that increasingly transcends traditional boundaries of religion and denomination—people wanting to learn from each other, *walking together, finding the way.*

SkyLight Paths, "Walking Together, Finding the Way," and colophon are trademarks of LongHill Partners, Inc., registered in the U.S. Patent and Trademark Office.

Walking Together, Finding the Way®
Published by SkyLight Paths Publishing
A Division of Longhill Partners, Inc.
Sunset Farm Offices, Route 4, P.O. Box 237
Woodstock, VT 05091
Tel: (802) 457-4000   Fax: (802) 457-4004
www.skylightpaths.com

To my husband, Gary,

who has been the greatest gift,

and who has walked through the gifts and losses of marriage

and raising three beloved sons,

Ian, Adam, and Graham

Contents

Acknowledgments

In the cold dark this past winter, I'd awake to a fire laid in the wood stove ready for the strike of a match to set it ablaze. My husband, Gary, gifted me with this warmth each day and the space and silence to write, tangible reminders of his love and support for which I am thankful beyond words.

I'm very grateful to Sister Teresa Jackson, OSB, who has hiked off-trail with me through the wild terrains of friendship, spiritual journey, and our North Idaho mountains, and who walked with me through every chapter with encouragement and challenge to go deeper. Thank you also to author Sandy Compton for insightful mentoring and to poet Jim Bodine for inviting me to "tell a story with passion."

My deep gratitude to Marcia Broucek, SkyLight Paths editor, for being a Gabriel voice in my life, for calling forth and seeing possibilities I could not see, and for accompaniment on this journey. My thank you to editor Nancy Fitzgerald, for graciously walking the last weeks of this book's journey with openness and patient guidance. Both have been blessings indeed.

Thank you to my family who allowed me to tell their stories and to the people who have privileged me by sharing their journeys through loss. You have trusted me with your vulnerability and tears as you traveled the desert of mourning, and you have also shared the gentle rain of healing and the gifts of life blossoming anew.

Prologue

For everything there is a season,
and a time for every matter under heaven:
a time to be born, and a time to die ...

Ecclesiastes 3:1–2

Valleys cup the low-lying fog. It silently swirls up into the mountain forest. Raindrops, brilliant as crystals with reflected cloud light, hang from pine needles. I breathe in creation's dampness, savoring its wet smell, its moist taste.

Then I see it. A mountain maple shrugs and a reddish gold leaf-fall cascades down the mountain. The tree sheds her stunning colors against the green darkness of pine and fir. Whoever knew letting go could be so breathtaking?

Yet there's also loneliness. The brilliant leaves are tinged brown. As they spiral downward, grief at something lost tugs at my heart. Just months ago, these same leaves burst out in spring's fresh green, growing large and full in summer's abundance. But now, the bouquet of clustered maple trunks bare themselves, turning toward winter's great night and six months of snow-covered white. Stunned by such melancholy beauty, I'm overwhelmed by loss.

How many moments of our daily lives are marked by such experiences of loss? A child awakens ill and in your concern, you cancel a busy workday of appointments. Your spouse loses a job. A trusted friend moves across the country. Achy muscles and splitting head announce you've caught the flat-on-your-back, weeklong flu that's been going around. You see more and more gray hair in the mirror. Your sister begins chemotherapy. Unexpected repairs deplete your savings. Your previously vital faith seems dry and brittle. An aging parent is diagnosed with Alzheimer's.

We continually walk through autumn times of our lives as each day brings losses. Fall regularly touches the vibrant leaves of our expectations and plans, causing them to blaze for a moment in tantalizing brightness, then turn brown and die. Life's constantly changing seasons invite us to shed our illusion of control and human-made security—or perhaps wrench it from us altogether. Like the trees of autumn, we, too, bare ourselves to being vulnerable and turn toward winter's night.

While mountain maple leaves do indeed die, the tree itself continues to live, even thrive. Nature's rhythms teach us profound lessons. We learn that fall's letting go and winter's fallow time inexorably turn into spring's exuberant new growth, which births summer abundance once more. Every year, we experience this cycle. Every year we are beckoned to walk its rhythm.

Every day, we are invited to personally experience these seasons. Autumn visits us when we must let go of something or someone. This pain-filled loss then turns us into winter's stark cold and mourning. Something dies, within us and without. And yet, in the fullness of time, from seemingly frozen ground, a green sprout of new spring growth pokes through the snow.

My mountain maple is large. Its shrublike base of many trunks spreads outward to cover ten feet of forest floor. Each year the trunks grow a little thicker, a little taller. And every year, tiny new saplings sprout around it. I welcome the maple's glorious spring and summer leafiness that provides shade, beauty, and indispensable food for rapid growth. But what about the maple's splendid autumnal shrug that sheds dazzling leaves on the forest floor? And what about its naked barrenness, stark branches silhouetted against gray sky throughout the apparent dead of winter? Doesn't growth also come from these seasons?

Touched by Loss

Who has not been touched by loss? From small everyday losses to the anguish of a loved one's death to the bewildering loss of ideals or beliefs to the painful loss of things and people we love—we are immersed in a continuing flow of loss. But at the same time, we're also submerged in an unending stream of life's immeasurable gifts.

This book is an invitation to awaken to life's enduring rhythm of sacred gift, of loss, and of renewing gift once again. It is astonishing how each of our days is saturated by gift and loss. These pages beckon us to be attentive to that rhythm.

I first learned life's strange rhythm of gift and loss as a child. Caring for injured birds and rabbits and seeing some of them die, moving away from my beloved tree house and creek, my grandfather's untimely death—I remember how sadness and grief were curiously mingled with life's joy and goodness. As an internal medicine physician, I witnessed loss sneak into my patients' lives as their bodies inexorably declined. And when practicing emergency medicine, loss ripped lives apart with split-second suddenness. An ongoing stream of my own personal losses continued—small everyday loss punctuated with occasional foundation-shaking loss that called everything into question. In the midst of it all, the sun still rose each morning, flowers still graced us all with beauty and fragrance, and people kept on loving and living. This life dance was an odd swirl of wondrous gift and agonizing loss.

In later years, as a pastor, I accompanied parishioners as they cried anguished tears of loss in my office and at police stations, hospitals, and gravesides. Now, as I sit with others in the sacred space of spiritual direction or as I lead retreats, I hear this inexorable rhythm of gift and loss repeat again and again. It permeates our lives in sunlit days and night's darkness, in the busyness of work and in the silence of prayer and meditation.

This book has been gestating throughout my life—and perhaps it has been gestating in your life, too. My dance and your dance with life's unending gift and loss will continue long after you've finished reading the last pages of this book. This dance, as all of life, is sacred. So where is the sacred in our losses? Where is the renewing gift after small, every-day losses and after huge, devastating ones?

We can easily see and welcome obvious gifts—the heady promise of springtime and the fruitful abundance of summer. But it's difficult to embrace the losses of autumn. Creation teaches us all too well that fall's losses inevitably turn into winter and some sort of dying.

The human voice has lamented these seasons of letting go through-out the ages. From Jewish psalmists comes a keening grief at loss that is timeless. It is as poignant today as it was thousands of years ago.

> *Save me, O God, for the waters have come up to my neck.*
> *I sink in deep mire, where there is no foothold;*
> *I have come into deep waters,*
> *and the flood sweeps over me.*
>
> PSALM 69:1–2

The psalmist's anguished cry is not flung into an indifferent cosmos. Rather, the unflinching wail of one drowning in grief is voiced in the sacred space of prayer. Losses and dyings are given to the deep mystery of God whose creation continually moves through unending cycles of autumn demise and winter death.

But just as autumn and winter possess their own desolate beauty, they may also bear sacred gifts. A lifetime of seasons teaches a hard-won wisdom that the entrance into spring's new growth is hidden deep within fall and winter.

> *Caught in the inevitable energy of packing and future planning, I am also bereft at leaving our home in Hawaii. Each morning I intently inhale plumeria's sweetness, listen to sounds of water, and memorize con-tours of the distant Waianae range. I want them forever*

etched in my being. The beauty of mango and papaya, ginger and star jasmine tugs at my heart. I mourn each good-bye as we pack.

There's a last sweet-scented breath before boarding, then I drink in my last sight of sparkling ocean surrounding reef runway. My heart breaks as the plane climbs past familiar palms, beach, and Diamond Head before we turn and head across the ocean. For years, I cry when hearing island music and cannot bear to return. And yet, over time, opportunities for our family—the reasons for which we moved—are gently given. We fall in love with new friends and places, while unexpected and astonishing new gifts come into our lives. I walk through my grief and in the fullness of time, our family returns for several weeks to savor once again island magic.

When we intentionally enter into our everyday walk through small losses, understanding their layers and how often we experience them, the terrain of larger loss is not completely unknown. Our walk through the valley of the shadow of death (Psalm 23:4) is not totally unfamiliar, alien, or terrifying, for we have walked some of this way before with our lesser losses. We can journey through this valley of difficult loss, for journey through it we must. And we can emerge on the other side, markedly changed, with hands open to receive profound, hard-won, life-renewing sacred gifts.

The arc of loss that stretches from our first to our last breath is the subject of this book. Come, journey with me through the essential losses of birth and growing-up years that mature us into adulthood. We will navigate the wisdom learned from insignificant losses that slip easily through our fingers while mining the hidden depths of painful losses of things and places. The rocky terrain of devastating loss of relationships and the heart-wrenching death of people we love will be traversed. We will explore the loss of well-being and safety that exposes our illusion of control and traverse the steep, dark slopes of loss of beliefs and faith. Finally, we will venture past midlife's turning point into our fear of the losses of aging and our own death.

This book is written for life travelers who journey the stark and difficult, yet strangely beautiful, landscape of letting go and dying to arrive at the courageously openhanded place where the gifts bestowed by such travel can be received. This is a continuing journey that winds through pain and liberation, grief and solace, growth and compassion to come home—home to a love so deep it surpasses comprehension.

This book is also written for those who accompany others through loss: spiritual directors and religious leaders, counselors and chaplains, medical and hospice caregivers, and good friends. This book can let us step back from this privileged work to appreciate the unending flow, as well as the breadth and depth of human loss. But the privilege of walking with others through loss cannot be separated from our own personal travels through loss. In fact, our journeying well and deeply through our own losses gives integrity and compassion to our guidance and companionship of others. This is the more difficult invitation to also allow this book to pull you into intentional exploration of your own losses.

The scope of the losses of our lives is best appreciated by engaging this book from front to back. But you can also choose to read specific chapters that speak most directly about your losses. Each chapter includes "Exploring Deeper" sections written for venturing deeper into your own losses. This is an invitation to not hold the book at arm's length for an intellectual read, but to set aside time to reflect on your own personal journey through loss. Consider keeping a journal to explore in words or art these parts of the book.

My parents planted me in Christian soil where my roots have eventually grown deep. From childhood bedtime stories to seminary, biblical narrative interweaves my life. But I've been accompanied along my journey by fellow travelers who are rooted in other traditions. Insightful rabbis and faithful Jewish friends, gentle Buddhists, lifelong Muslims, and particularly loving, passionate Sufis have befriended me.

They have walked alongside me and generously shared wisdom, scripture, meditation, and prayer. While I'm grounded in the soil of Christianity, my fellow Jewish, Muslim, and Buddhist wayfarers have also opened my eyes to this present moment and the sacred ground upon which we walk our lives.

This book is an invitation to be attentive to that sacred ground. It is a beckoning to be aware of life's abundant gifts, difficult losses, and renewing gifts that are interwoven into this pilgrimage we call life.

The Human Tapestry

As a deer longs for flowing streams,
so my soul longs for you, O God.

Psalm 42:1

God, you have made us for yourself,
and our hearts are restless till they find their
rest in you ....

St. Augustine of Hippo

An eerie sound, primal and wild, draws me out into the moonlit snow to listen. Hair tingles on the back of my neck and a shiver traces my spine. In winter's long night, coyotes howl in the cold of our north country home.

Coyote wails disturb me. They come from another realm, a realm I fear to acknowledge. Coyote howls pull me from my warm home and arouse a primitive excitement of something dangerous within me. I glimpse a deep, fearful kinship with their cries.

One summer night near Ganado, Arizona, a Navajo man joins me looking at the stars. The sun-wrinkled elder asks if I know the story of Coyote and starlight. When I shake my head, he begins to speak softly into the Navajo Nationland night.

Long ago, before two-leggeds walked the earth, there were no stars in the night sky. The animals cannot see in the darkness. They ask Great Spirit for help. Great Spirit picks up a shining stone from a running stream and puts it in the sky where it becomes a star. Great Spirit invites the animals to gather shining stones and place them in the sky, making bright pictures of themselves. The animals begin excitedly, but soon grow tired.

So they ask Coyote, who has not done any work, to finish their pictures. Coyote, thinking he is the wisest of all animals, envisions creating the biggest, brightest picture of them all in the sky—that of Coyote! Not wanting to waste time finishing the other animals' pictures, he takes their collected stones and flings them up into the dark sky. Wildly scattering, they form stars everywhere but don't complete any images.

Too late, Coyote realizes that in his haste, he has forgotten to save any stones for his own magnificent self-portrait. Furious, Coyote begins to howl into the night, wailing into the cosmos at the loss of his grand sky-image in the heavens.

Navajo wisdom understands the effect of coyote cries on the human spirit. Their mournful wails raise goose bumps on my skin and arouse a deeply rooted, primal yearning for something irretrievably lost. What is lost, I do not know. I only know that the object of this loss is hidden in the dust of the past. A longing woven deep in my being underpins my days and nights. While busyness of my waking hours masks this longing, it rises to the surface in the solitude and silence of long winter nights when coyotes howl.

Missing Threads

Scientists say coyotes howl to gather their pack, calling others back together. This is what we humans do, too, when we've lost someone.

We yearn to reconnect, to be close once again. Our longing propels us to retrace our steps, to put ourselves in that place where we were last together. If we do not see the missing one, then we call out in hope that the person will hear us and be drawn back to us. Our longing to see a face, to hear a voice, to touch a hand intensifies as we realize the enormity of our loss and our yearning.

Religion and spirituality professor Barbara Brown Taylor's *The Preaching Life* contains an evocative scene.

> My parents and I lived in rural Kansas, in a tract house on an old cornfield where the west wind blew so hard that everything in the yard grew toward Missouri.... Behind our small home was a patio, a swing set, and a long view to the east, where a convent sat in the distance like an oasis in the broom grass. One evening, my mother says, she missed me in the house and found me out there, facing the convent and calling "Nino!" at the top of my lungs. No one knew who Nino was, least of all me, but for some time I called him every day at dusk, singing his name across the dark field with the west wind in my hair and the setting sun at my back.[1]

Young Barbara doesn't recognize the name she calls. She cannot articulate that for which she yearns. But in the wide expanse of sky and earth, she cries out for someone who is missing, her words carried aloft by the wind.

Isn't this the truth of our existence? At root in the dark of night, when the day's chaos is over and we are alone in the quiet, we become aware of a deep yearning that underlies our existence. Sometimes this longing even breaks into our hectic days. When life is unpredictable and the day as we planned it shifts beneath our feet, a primordial anxiety awakens within us. We are filled with feeling that somehow a thread has been pulled and the tapestry of our lives is incomplete.

We yearn for ... what? Do we desire a peace that eludes us, a calm to assuage our restlessness, a love that will anchor us amidst life's storms, the certainty of a safe harbor? Is this a surface taste of a deeper hunger hidden below our consciousness—an ancient longing given voice in a cry as primal as a coyote's howl or as wistful as a small child calling into the wind?

Applied philosopher Thomas Attig speaks of life as a weaving in *Meaning Reconstruction and the Experience of Loss*:

> Our life stories ... are filled with weaving and reweaving of webs of connection, patterns of caring in which we find and make meaning. Bereavement strikes a blow to those webs.... The weaves of our daily life patterns are in tatters.[2]

When a mysterious thread is missing from the very core of our lives, we are left to wail or call our ancient longing into the darkening night.

Birthed into Separateness

When our first grandchild is born, nine months of my son and daughter-in-law's pregnant waiting could not prepare me for this moment. Sleeping newborns embody a deep wisdom in their exquisite faces and bring even the most gregarious among us to a hushed, awe-filled silence. They are so astoundingly perfect, so naturally who they are. Stunned by the breathtaking beauty of this newborn, I marvel at the wonder of a grandchild. How can this be? Tiny Alec's innocence is devoid of masks, pretense, or ill-fitting adaptive behaviors. I gaze at him, mesmerized. Surely this tiny sleeping one is a glimpse into the face of God.

Even young children sense the sacred in a newborn, as biblical scholar Marcus Borg tells so beautifully in this story in *The Heart of Christianity*:

> A three-year-old little girl was very excited that her mother was pregnant and that she would soon have a new brother or sister. Within a few hours of the parents bringing a new baby boy home from the hospital, the girl made a request: she wanted to be alone with her new brother in his room with

the door shut. Her insistence about being alone with the baby with the door closed made her parents a bit uneasy, but then they remembered that they had installed an intercom system in anticipation of the baby's arrival, so they realized they could let their daughter do this, and if they heard the slightest indication that anything strange was happening, they could be in the baby's room in an instant.

So they let the little girl go into the baby's room, shut the door and raced to the intercom listening station. They heard their daughter's footsteps moving across the baby's room, imagined her standing over the baby's crib, and then they heard her saying to her three-day-old brother, "Tell me about God—I've almost forgotten."[3]

Two-day-old Alec is unaware of emerging from a sacred knowing, or of beginning to lose that sense of knowing. He is not consciously aware of missing anything ... yet. Of course, he cries when he is hungry for warm milk and the comfort of his mother's breast. But once he is sated, he sleeps in deep stillness. His body limp, the last drops of milk drooling carelessly out the corner of his mouth, he is wondrous in his profound contentment.

Fed, held, and loved, Alec is unaware of the momentousness of having been pushed out of the womb, his umbilical cord severed. He is blissfully unconscious of his birthed separateness, of understanding that he and his mother are not one. Thriving on his parents' love and nurture, he embarks on the lifelong journey of becoming the individual we call Alec.

The weaving of Alec's life tapestry is only beginning. He does not yet call out a name to the wind in response to deep, unarticulated longing. Nor is he old enough to coyote-howl into moonlit nights. But someday, sometime, he will become aware of a deep yearning for something that seems forever lost, a yearning that was born at the watershed moment of his birth.

This is not a new story. Ancient narratives weave tapestries that describe other wombs and other births into physical separateness. They also speak of a profound longing to return. The garden-womb of Eden, described in the opening chapters of the Bible, has everything to nourish newly conceived man and woman: sustaining food and water, beauty and comfort and safety, times of man and woman being one, and a natural closeness with God strolling the garden.

But there is also that tree in the very center of the garden, which the narrative tells us is "good for food ... a delight to the eyes ... [and] desired to make one wise" (Genesis 3:6). The story begins with a warning about this tree: God warns of death to anyone who eats its fruit.

When the woman and man eat the forbidden fruit, they do not physically die. Rather, there is a birth of sorts as their eyes are opened. But with this birth is also great loss. Something does indeed die. The woman and man lose their innocence, become aware that they, their life, and their bodies are fully exposed to God. They no longer feel at ease on garden strolls with God coming upon them unexpectedly. They are anxious about God seeing them just as they are. So they run from ingenuous closeness with God to hide in newfound separateness. A post-Eden way of being is birthed and the idyll of Eden's garden is eternally lost. Now it is God who calls into the wind, "Where are you?" (Genesis 3:9).

Uprooted, torn from the garden, a forever ache—a primal loss—is born in humankind. This ache is a natal yearning to be planted once again in the garden's soil, to be protected in Eden's amniotic waters, to live with God in naked vulnerability.

Coming Home to God

There is more to this story, a foundational narrative that overarches all primal loss and longing: "In the beginning ... a wind from God swept over the face of the waters" (Genesis 1:1–2).

In the beginning God exhales in the darkness of a not-yet cosmos. Divine breath sends matter expanding outward to form the universe. But this is not a singular event. Sacred wind persists in sweeping over the waters of each not-yet moment.

In this divine out-breathing, we are created in sacred love. And in the way of creatures, we are conceived in human love. Love is deep-woven into our developing bones and sinews, our emergent mind and heart, from the beginning. If anything is our birthright, it is love.

Is this the root of our yearning? Do we long for the One who breathes us into life? Deep within our being, do we ache for our sacred birthright of love?

This God-longing draws us out to listen as the coyote's mournful wails give voice to the ache within us. Inside our competent, self-assured adult is a hunger. Amidst life's unknowns and losses, we long for divine presence. Our small human voices call into life's darkening nights for the One we've lost. It is this birthright love, this first unconscious experience of divine love that echoes faintly for the three-year-old girl as she gazes on her newborn brother. "Tell me about God, I've almost forgotten," she whispers to the tiny baby boy.

Ever so vaguely within us is memory of Eden's closeness with an earlier love. Created in divine image, our birth east of Eden seems to tear us from a life of oneness in God. Our first taste of sacred love sparks an insatiable longing. When life turns upside down in the nighttime of uncertainty and loss, we long to be loved again just as we are, without pretense or cover-up. Our true identity is revealed in this love. We are the "beloved."

This compass-setting longing for God turns us again and again toward reweaving awareness of the divine presence back into the tapestry of our lives. We strain to find the threads to remember the timbre of God's voice so we can listen for it amidst the world's cacophony. We search for memory of God's face, seeking it in all we see. Longing is the warp thread upon which our life tapestry is woven.

We glimpse this love sometimes in moments of stillness or in our experience of ordinary, extraordinary human love. But there is no "cure" for our God-homesickness, for this primal experience of seeming loss. There is only our continual yearning.

We cannot crawl back into the womb from which we have been born. We cannot reenter the long-ago bliss of our mother's belly. We cannot regress into a newborn's psychological womb of perceived oneness with our mother. And biblical narrative tells us the way back to the Eden-womb, ingenuous life with God in the garden is sealed.

Like a coyote wailing in the night, subsequent losses in our lives will recall us to our primal, intrinsic longing for God. As we navigate through life's losses, we hear echoes of our divine homesickness. Everyday, insignificant loss, as well as extraordinary loss, plunge us into the cold undercurrents of our seeming loss of sacred presence. We emerge sputtering and shivering, feeling vulnerable and alone.

The deep interconnectedness of daily loss with our foundational yearning for God has something to show us. Our lifelong pilgrimage through loss can teach us to recognize cairns along the way, markers that can guide us. Perhaps our everyday journey through loss can even show us the way home.

Being Aware

Primal longings of the human spirit are expressed in varied ways. Narratives about coyotes howling, a little girl calling into the night, and birth experiences explore humankind's inner sense of sacred yearning.

Awareness of our own longing comes in different ways. Specific, tangible losses such as a divorce, a death, or the loss of a job often awaken us to deeper rhythms of loss and underlying yearning in our lives.

Deep-seated, sacred longing can also be subtle, even disguised. It may manifest as restlessness, as a persistent urge to move, to change, to veer off onto a different course. We may have an inkling that all is not quite right in our lives, that something is amiss. We may be impelled to seek that which is missing and to search for that which we cannot name. Anxiety or unease can herald the surfacing of this yearning. After a life crisis, or in our midlife, we can painfully feel the ground beneath our feet shift. Belongings, beliefs, and vocation for which we've worked so hard may no longer nourish us or evoke our passion. We may feel that life has lost meaning.

When we are alert, we awaken to a vague yet insistent sense of longing for something lost. Think of this as an invitation to stop and look at life anew. We're beckoned to pause our headlong rush into the next moment and to be quiet, to listen deeply, to become attentive to our yearnings. As we awake to ancient longings, we may hear the coyote howl or our own voice call into the night seeking wholeness, completeness, oneness.

We may even faintly hear God's voice calling to us, "Where are you?"

Spiritual Practice
BREATH PRAYER

There are many practices, ancient wisdom from previous spiritual travelers, that can enhance our mindfulness and lead us into awareness. These practices gently turn us from being blown one way, then another, by our human-made agendas and frenetic concerns, to settle us into a deeper attentiveness.

The first thing we do at birth is take our initial breath. And the last thing we do at death is to exhale our final breath. Intentional awareness of something as simple as breathing grounds us in the wonder of life. Focus upon our current breath brings us into this present moment. The word for God's Spirit in Hebrew scripture, *Ruach*, pertains to breath. The ancient Christian practice of praying without ceasing often involves praying with the rhythm of breathing. Sitting awareness of breathing is practiced in yoga and Buddhist meditation.

- Find a quiet place. Set this time aside. Close the door, turn off the computer and phone. Settle into the silence.
- Slow down. Relax.
- One by one, remember your undone tasks. Visualize laying them down, letting them rest unfinished. Think of people or situations that concern you. Hold them gently in your hands, then release them to God. Rest in the gift of this space, this time.
- Be aware of your breathing. What is the rate of your breaths? Are they shallow or deep?
- Take a long, slow breath. Notice the breath begins in your nostrils, expands your chest, then pushes out your stomach. Pause at the top of your breath. Then exhale slowly. Pause at the bottom of your breath. Continue these long, slow breaths.
- Be fully present in this moment, attentive to life-giving breath flowing in and out of you. You may also couple prayer words to your breathing in and breathing out.

As you spend time in silence and with "being" rather than "doing," you become comfortable with the practice and sink gratefully into daily moments of quiet.

What is it like to have time without tasks or expectations? What is it like to be quiet, to slow down?

Exploring Deeper

Our daily lives may be so full and busy that we have little space to hear deeper yearnings. Truth be told, we may pack our days to overflowing precisely to avoid awareness of inner longing. We can suppress this sense of a missing thread in our lives with a frenetic pace, too many activities, and the constant presence of others. If we fall into bed exhausted, we avoid the echoes calling in the depths of night that urge us to find the missing strands.

This yearning is disquieting. It calls for change in our lives. It calls into question how we live our days, our beliefs, our perception of the universe and our place in it. This longing overturns our understanding of our own identity—and that of God. Reflect on your own life in relationship to what you've just read in this chapter. Do you overfill your days to avoid being alone? Is something not quite right in your life, or have you lost direction or meaning? Do you crave something more, or ache for something you cannot name?

To be aware of inner longings, we need to intentionally clear a space in our busyness. When we hold open a protected, empty place, we are finally able to hear subtle whispers. As we wait in silence, we become attentive to deeper yearnings that surface.

Each exercise beckons a gentle, personal look at your life. Where does the chapter's exploration of loss intersect with your experience? Where have you walked this journey already?

Enter into this deeper exploration at whatever level seems appropriate. You may want to keep a notebook handy to explore further in words or art.

You could write or draw your own prayer or free verse in the pages of your notebook.

Longing

a deep gnawing with sharp teeth
eats at my soul
dull or sharp it never leaves but whispers and
*   shouts*
for my attention
listen it says
listen, I am speaking your truth
do not fear the silence,
the dark whispers
they are the God breath of new life.

Sister Teresa Jackson, OSB

Open Up to Primal Longings and Loss

The following exercises help us listen and become aware of inner stirrings. It is vital not to rush through these exercises.

Enter into these exercises in a comfortable place after you are quieted—perhaps after breath prayer. Listen for longings that are submerged, avoided, or missed beneath your busyness. You can continue this exercise over time, to cultivate a heightened alertness to what is happening deep inside.

- What do you experience in moments of quiet, silent attentiveness? What thoughts, feelings, and emotions surface?
- Is there any sense of incompleteness—of being separate, alone, or vulnerable? Are you aware of restlessness or unease? Do you yearn for something that seems to be missing?
- Have you noticed these feelings or thoughts before? How did you respond?
- Sit with these thoughts or feelings.
- Stay with whatever surfaces. Do not try to explain or rationalize. Don't try to understand. Just be attentive to whatever rises up in this time.

Exploring with Art

Longings rooted below the level of conscious thought can emerge through creative endeavors. You can access deep yearnings in surprising ways through the symbolic language of poetry and prayer, color, and shape. This is not about producing a finished piece of writing or art, but about listening deeply to what emerges in the creative process. This can be surprisingly insightful—particularly if these are new practices for you.

- Take a piece of loosely woven material like burlap or muslin. Appreciate the interweaving threads as they loop over and under each other to create a whole. Pull one thread. Is it difficult? Is there resistance, tension, puckering? Describe the cloth after the thread is completely pulled out.
- Write, draw, or color what "longing" means to you. You could make a montage of words written in different colors and styles scattered over a page, or write a poem or prayer free-style and unstructured. You can draw longing or unreservedly swirl the colors of yearning on a paper.
- What thoughts and feelings arise?
- Spend time with what emerges. Leave the material or paper in your quiet space to ponder and pray with it in days ahead.

Pray

Settle me into this moment,
this once-in-a-lifetime moment, O God.
Quiet me.
Make me still.

Give me courage to sit with my longings.
Let me hear your whisper
calling me,
beneath the surface
to your undercurrents.
Amen

2

Birth Pangs and Passages

A visitor to famous Polish Rabbi Hafez Hayyim was
astonished to see the rabbi's home was a small room
completely bare except for books.

"Rabbi, where is your furniture?"

"Where is yours?" asked the rabbi.

"Mine? But I'm only a visitor here."

"So am I," said the rabbi.

from Stories of the Spirit, Stories of the Heart[1]

In the beginning when God created the heavens and
the earth, the earth was a formless void and darkness
covered the face of the deep, while a wind from God
swept over the face of the waters.

Genesis 1:1–2

To become attentive to the losses of our everyday lives, we need to
start at the very beginning.

In the beginning, darkness covers the face of the deep. Half-
strands of mother's DNA and half-strands of father's DNA, each separate and incomplete, spiral around each other. God exhales and a
spirit-filled wind sweeps over the waters. Separate DNA strands join

15

together, nucleotide to nucleotide, and form a complete DNA coil. A new life is conceived.

Newly created, we are fresh and unknown. And yet, the gift of this original melody that is our self is composed of notes that are very familiar. We have Daddy's eyes, Mommy's hands, Grandma's mouth, Great-grandpa's hair. Novel and innovative, we are fashioned from ancient sources. We are composed of stardust, knit together from the same primordial particles that formed the universe from the very beginning. Brand spanking new, we are also as old as creation itself.

Birth and Loss

Have you ever wondered about your life before birth? I invite you to imaginatively journey into the hidden womb-world where we develop. Thousands of years ago, the psalmist could only prayerfully imagine this space. "You who formed my inward parts; you knit me together in my mother's womb ... when I was being made in secret" (Psalm 139:13, 15).

Here, we receive the sacred gift of life. Here, we also first experience loss.

Today, science lets us glimpse into the womb. Suspended in amniotic fluid, we are swaddled in an environment that supplies our every need. The womb's watery cocoon buffers life's jolts. The impact as mother jogs, dances, or slips on an icy walk is softened, muted to shield us from life's abrupt knocks. The constant temperature is ideal, so we do not know hot or cold. Our life-giving placenta provides nourishment, so that we are unaware of hunger. It even provides us with oxygen, as we have not yet begun to breathe.

Our first world is not silent. We hear the low timbre of father's voice, the melody of mother singing, the crash of a dropped dish. These muffled sounds punctuate the all-encompassing pulse of mother's beating heart. We hear her blood surge forward, then subside, speeding up with movement or excitement and restfully slowing with relaxation and sleep. Daytime brings sound and activity; night is quiet. We are introduced in a tamped-down way to life's rhythm of ebb and flow.

We thrive, grow; soon we fill our space completely. Our body stretches its muscular cradle until there is little room to kick or turn anymore. We are now constricted by our protective home. Our nourishing placenta nears the end of its life span, no longer able to furnish our growing needs. Mother's body is weary and slow-moving from our size and weight. The extraordinary gift of life in the womb has been given. It is time to be born.

There is "a time to be born, and a time to die," wisdom writer Ecclesiastes tells us in the Hebrew scriptures (Ecclesiastes 3.2). On first reading, this sentence seems to portray borning times as very different from dying times. On the surface, birth and death appear to be polar opposites, mutually exclusive experiences. But are they so different?

Poised on the threshold of birth, what is about to happen? The emergence of new life is a wondrous gift, eagerly anticipated and celebrated with joy. But to be born, what must change, what must be lost? Or using Ecclesiastes' words, what must die for birth to happen?

Birth precipitates one of the most dramatic, all-encompassing changes we'll ever experience in life. (The other cataclysmic change is our physical death at the distal end of life.) At birth, we lose the gift of the womb's nurturing shelter. Our gentle float in warm water, cushioned from harsh sound, physical jolting, and temperature extremes is lost. Our insulation from hunger is gone. Our intimate life within mother's life, our one existence dies. The overarching sound of her heartbeat ends.

It begins innocently enough with the same gentle "practice" contractions we've experienced in recent weeks. But this time, something new happens. Ever creating, divine wind moves again over the waters in the womb's darkness. Contractions come closer and closer together and compress us hard. They relentlessly constrict our uterine world and force us down into an even narrower space. When our amniotic sac breaks, the buffer between us and the world drains away in a gush of fluid.

In the fullness of time, we are pushed out, dripping wet amidst the primal cries of our mother.

Coming from the womb, we are assaulted by the outside world. We have never experienced such intense light, such harsh noise, such cold. We must take our first breath. And then another, and another. The circulation of blood in our fetal heart must alter to become the circulation of an air-breathing infant. For the first time, we cry out loud. Our umbilical cord is severed; we learn hunger and must suck our food. We no longer live inside mother's life, but are birthed an unmistakably separate person. We are taken from our mother to be cleaned, weighed, and examined.

The magnitude of what we have lost is impossible to articulate.

And yet, we also experience the gentle, warm hands of caring people who dry us and wrap us in warm blankets and lay us upon our mother, our skin touching her skin. We are given into mother's awed embrace and may have our first opportunity to suck at her breast. We hear in a new way father's familiar voice and feel his caress. These sacred gifts are the first taste of our birthright of love.

The magnitude of what we have been given is impossible to articulate.

We have no choice in this birthing. We do not choose to accept the wondrous gift of separate life. We have no option whether to experience the inescapable loss. We are born. And the death of all we have known walks hand in hand with the birth of everything we will know.

From a physical perspective, birth is nonnegotiable. The womb, a vital gift for nine months of gestational growth, now limits us. We have outgrown our life-giving home; to stay would mean certain death. Birth must happen for us to continue to live and grow.

This first birthing is our primary experience of an archetypal pattern that will repeat again and again throughout life. In the birth cries of every mother echoes the ancient truth that new birth and growth always entails loss, often painful loss. We outgrow previous gifts, even wondrous, sacred gifts that were crucial to nourish our lives. This primal pattern of loss being essential to new birth will undergird all our days and years of life.

Ecclesiastes' words sound in all birthing cries. But the wisdom of life's experience reveals something surprising. Birth and death, seemingly quite separate experiences, are intricately related, even yoked together. The times to be born are also the times to die. They are two sides of the same experience—for anything new to be born, something must die.

Birthed Again

Like our first birthing, many of our subsequent losses are not only inescapable but crucial for our continued life and growth. These later birthings mean the loss of previous gifts whose blessings have been fully received. Life's recurring rhythm of sacred gift, its loss, and new gift begins even before we are aware.

Our newborn self is severed from mother when our umbilical cord is severed. We are laid upon mother's tummy while the cord is held for father to cut. In adult eyes, this cut decisively separates baby from mother. But as newborns, we are unable (perhaps mercifully) to recognize this. Blissfully unaware of the enormity of our birth, we cannot yet distinguish mother's warmth and embrace, her breast and milk, from our infant self. In the haze of our newborn world, mother's provision of sustenance and safety seems part of us. We are temporarily spared the terror of fully experiencing our vulnerable separateness. It will take the decades of childhood and adolescence to awake and claim our individuality. Echoes of this process will continue through adulthood.

The recurring pattern of loss making way for new birth begins afresh. As the womb environment became constrictive, so our newborn perception of idyllic unity with mother will also limit us. Another loss and another birth must happen to set us on our next step on the long journey of growing into our unique selves.

Within the first six months of life, when our cries are not immediately answered, or when they are answered in an unexpected way, we gradually realize that mother and father are separate from us. Child psychiatrist and analyst Margaret Mahler labels this gradual awareness of being separate as our "psychological birth" or "hatching." In *The Psychological Birth of the Human Infant: Symbiosis and Individuation*, Mahler writes:

> The biological birth of the human infant and the psychological birth of the individual are not coincident in time. The former is a dramatic, observable and well-circumscribed event; the latter, a slowly unfolding intrapsychic process. Like any intrapsychic process, this one reverberates through the life cycle. It is never finished; it remains always active; new phases of the life cycle see new derivatives of the earliest processes still at work.[2]

Most of the hard work of this process is completed by the time a child has reached his third birthday.

Psychological birth begins as our blurry newborn world takes form and shape. Objects and people appear, different from one another and from ourselves. Boundaries emerge. Here I am. And there you are. Only from this developing stance as an individual can we now enter the life-dance of interacting with others and learn the language of relationship. We recognize a smile, and smile back in turn. Father speaks to us, and we mimic him by "talking" in wordless baby utterances. We distinguish faces of people we know from those of strangers and respond selectively to those who are close to us. We learn to roll over and move away from our parents.

With this psychological birth, of course, comes loss. As our baby mind begins to recognize physical separateness, we lose our blissful oneness with our world. In ever-progressive degrees, we lose our first artless experience of union in exchange for claiming the gift of growing into our individual selves. The headwaters of a poignant lifelong journey flow from here.

Is this watershed turning from innocent oneness into awareness of being separate the beginning of our "forgetting"? We hear a three-year-old girl's whispered voice asking a newborn baby about God. She's now old enough and separate enough to have almost forgotten sacred presence, breathtakingly close. She is old enough and separate enough to yearn for divine love.

The Cycle Continues

Although the umbilical cord has been cut and we've left behind perceived oneness with mother to enter the astonishing world of relationship, we still need lifelines to others, so we begin to form new psychological, social, and spiritual umbilical cords. These attachments gift us with human bonds that nourish us in crucial ways. We become tightly attached to those who are lovingly present to give us food and warmth, cuddling, and playfulness.

The loss of both the womb and our Eden-like oneness lets us receive an amazing gift. From our newly accepted stance as a separate individual, from our entrance into back-and-forth relationships, we awaken to love. We become aware of the taste and feel and look and sound of love.

We love because we were loved first.

Only as a separate individual can we receive and give love. Basking in the love of those close to us, we now join the blessed dance of loving back. Our experience of human love is also a glimpse into the encompassing divine love that is our birthright. Through our family's love, we taste the flavor of sacred love that will always leave us hungering for more.

When Mommy vanishes around the corner of the kitchen island, nine-month-old Alec follows her at a fast crawl. He rounds the corner, but she's nowhere to be seen. He quickly crawls around the next corner, but still no Mommy. He sits, perplexed. She's gone. But then Mommy leaps out from the other direction, and they dissolve in a giggle-and-hug reunion. "Okay, I get this,"

Alec thinks. He quickly learns the game and stops at each corner to listen and look both directions for Mommy. Even though he can't see her, he learns that neither she nor her love are gone.

Versions of the baby game of peek-a-boo are our first intentional lesson in learning that people haven't fallen off the earth just because we can't touch, see, or hear them. Somehow people continue to exist outside our baby world, and their love persists even in absence.

As small babies, we learn an ancient choreography of healthy relationship between individuals. But in the fullness of time, we will outgrow these ties in their infant and childhood forms. There will be successive births as we mature, and our childhood attachments will be cut to deliver our increasingly separate selves.

We continually test how far love extends by increasing our "safe" distance from our parents. Is there a peek-a-boo boundary beyond which we are forever separated from the one we love? Gleefully, we toddle away with heady independence for wildly exciting forays into the world. Then we stop. Looking back at our distance, our aloneness, and our terrifying vulnerability, we abandon audacious exploration and run back for reassuring cuddles. By our third birthday, we have navigated the loss of needing our parents infant-close and are comfortable with enough distance to exist in three-year-old separateness. Our childhood ties to our parents are not severed in one decisive action, but pulled and stretched throughout our growing-up years until their importance diminishes and we can let them go.

Like a compelling drumbeat, the rhythm of this oddly beautiful dance of birth, loss, and new birth continues in our school years. Each independent step into becoming an individual is founded on loss of parental intimacy. Persistently tugging at childhood umbilical cords, we leave home for preschool, day trips with friends, and our first overnight. Joining the band, we stay after school; we go out on dates and spend weekend time with friends. We toddle, walk, bicycle, take the school bus, and eventually drive away from our parents. As adults we continue to form vital, healthy attachments. We also continue to experience their loss. Relationships, situations, understandings, and beliefs that are crucial for our growth in one stage of life become constrictive as we mature. We repeatedly outgrow that which was essential and nourishing earlier in our lives. For further growth and maturation to happen, we must leave them behind. The cadence of sacred gift, loss, and new gift repeats.

Leaving Home

Powerful emotions lurk by our home's front door. We are first carried across the threshold as a blanket-wrapped infant. Through this door we continue to come home from the outside world of play, school, friendships, life's challenges and frictions. "Ah," we say gratefully, "we're home."

But doors are powerful, ambivalent passages. Through this door we also leave home for the wonder and mystery of the unknown world. Each significant step over the doorsill, away from the love-security-familiarity of home and into the unfamiliar "out there" world, tips over conflicting front-door emotions. Second thoughts and boomerang feelings drench us on our way out.

Wearing squeaky new shoes that seem too big, we struggle with our new backpack. "Ready?" we're asked. We stand uncertainly by the door, lip quavering and eyes filling with tears. Gently taking our small hand, our parent leads us out the door to the "big" school on our first day of kindergarten.

Finally we're old enough for the fun of summer camp. Mom helps us pack and fixes us a special breakfast on the day we're to leave. But we don't feel like eating. It takes forever to get dressed. We look longingly around our room at favorite toys and beloved books. Standing by the front door, we tell our parents we don't really want to go to camp.

After months of excited planning, our long-awaited eighth-grade school trip arrives at last. We quickly dress in the dark for our early morning departure and toss a last-minute toothbrush into our carefully packed duffle bag. But we pause at the door, a strange feeling in our stomach. Inside our big middle-school body, an uncertain kindergartner's eyes fill with tears as we once again prepare to leave home.

There is always loss in these leave-takings. Every successive birth of ourselves is painful, for it cuts deep to let go of that which has nourished us. When we walk out that door, we leave behind the gift of home where our parents' love is tangible in the smell of our favorite supper and endless games of catch. We walk away from home's safety and our parents' hugs. We leave to venture further than we've ever been before.

But if we are to grow into an independent adult, we must continue to walk out the front door. From a three-year-old who can't open the door, to a first grader who struggles with the handle, to a high schooler who nonchalantly leaves the door open on the way out, we keep leaving home. Each breathtaking excursion into independence is bolder, riskier than any previous one. We learn there are indeed challenges out there, but we also experience astounding new sights, astonishing people, and a universe opening before us.

Every venture through this door stretches us a little further and prepares us for the watershed day when we leave home for good. In *All Our Losses, All Our Griefs: Resources for Pastoral Care,* pastoral care experts Kenneth Mitchell and Herbert Anderson write, "Growing up and leaving home involves relationship loss, material loss, intrapsychic loss, systemic loss, and role loss ... leaving home is one of the most powerful and critical loss events any human being undergoes."[3]

As we graduate from high school and prepare to head off to college, a new job, volunteer or military service, some people give us significant gifts for the trip. This pivotal life passage is marked with nearly as much anticipation and preparation as our birth many years ago. This is indeed another birth.

When the day of our leave-taking arrives, we ferry boxes to the car, walking back and forth through the front door. Our movement stitches the known of childhood's past to the unknown of adulthood's future. Box after box empties the room until only its shell remains with left-behind childhood mementoes. Or we may leave behind nearly everything, taking only one or two suitcases if we're taking a bus, train, or airplane to our new home. The ambivalence of this good-bye swirls in a gut-wrenching mix of excitement and fear about the unknown future.

No childhood is perfect. Difficult waters of bruising childhood experiences can run underneath these emotions. We all have scars. Many are well healed; some are still a little tender, but mending; while a few deep wounds have only the tenuous cover of a thin, adolescent scab. We desperately want to leave behind these wounds and memories. But they come with us, unwanted secret stowaways we would never choose to pack. When we walk out the door this time, we carry with us the awful truth that people get hurt and life isn't fair.

Our parent calls from downstairs. It's time.

We've anticipated this independence day for months. But we hadn't realized the enormity of our loss on this birthing day. The uncertain, teary-eyed kindergarten-elementary-middle-school kid comes with us as we cross the threshold.

Sacred wind ruffles the waters as we approach the front door. No one takes our hand. It's time to let go of childhood. We cannot know what we'll receive in return.

We pull the door closed behind us and drive away.

When we say good-bye to our parents, they speak words of endearment and encouragement. We mumble, "Thank you, I love you," and desperately hope tears do not betray us. There's a last lingering hug, and after eighteen years, we turn to go our separate ways.

It's over. And it's beginning. Birth-loss pounds the rhythm.

The magnitude of what we have lost is enormous.

And yet, we soon meet others, also newly separated, and we share new experiences together. We put our tattered childhood blanket on the bed (concealed under our new adult cover), tack posters on the walls, and tape strings of twinkle lights on the ceiling. We learn to not forget so many things and to plan ahead. We receive the gift of knowledge, skill, and confidence as we navigate through our first months.

The magnitude of what we have been given is monumental.

We discover our family connection isn't completely severed. Balancing between distance and closeness, we are buoyed by brief parental visits and occasional care packages. What began eighteen years ago with a decisive cut of our umbilical cord has largely finished in this hard-won culmination of our journey into selfhood.

We are born.

THE BUS STATION

The chair that's a little too low is still at the desk, and the old ink stain is faintly visible on the carpet. The quirky short closets in the alcove seem even smaller. Dormer windows that used to look down on a spindly sweet gum tree now look straight into the belly of the tree with its sturdy branches. All of this is so familiar, yet strangely distant. Just like the teenager I used to be. I pick up my bag.

Like old times, I ride in the back seat of my parents' car to the bus station. Alongside the cocked-up doors of the bus's luggage compartment, the driver takes my scuffed bag. Hugs all around; Mom and Dad whisper, "We love you." How many good-byes have we said?

Through the bus window, my parents look old. When did gray sprinkle their hair? They wait patiently on the sidewalk. I don't usually return home midsemester. But this is my last semester before I move cross-country for medical school.

As the bus pulls away, tears fill Mom's eyes, and Dad's face is tight with emotion. My stomach tenses, my eyes sting. I see my room again—the room Dad finished and painted my favorite pale yellow. Childhood memories parade in kaleidoscope succession. Mom is silhouetted in the window as she stitches my new curtains. Dad holds long nails between his teeth while he hammers my tree house into place. Mom says, "Hold still!" as she pins the hem on my new dress; Dad holds my hand as he finds our Sunday concert seats. Mom "grown-up" chats with me on swivel seats at the lunch counter. Dad talks me down a terrifying ski slope.

Grief stuns me. Why, at the age of twenty-one, and after all our good-byes, is this happening?

Of course, another good-bye is coming as I move further from home. But there's more. Somehow, my parents' aging—even as I grow older—isn't part of the script. We all have unchanging parts in this decades-long, growing-up saga. I stretch my childhood ties, unfurl wings and fly way. They tend home fires, stalwart and resolute protector-nurturers.

But now I see my parents have let go of their parental roles and turned to embrace their later years. Neither yesterday's parents nor yesterday's child live in the house anymore. My childhood home-world has passed, and the

*final curtain on this leaving-home story is resolutely
brought down.*

We have all left home.

*We all have new roles in a new narrative. The bus
puts miles between me and home. As I taste bittersweet
finality, tears begin to fall. I cry for the sweetness of
being rocked when my knee was skinned and for protec-
tion from childhood bullies. I mourn mountain hikes
and trumpet-piano duets with my dad, sewing lessons
and laughter with my mom. My parents knew this ended
long before I did. Mom's tears and Dad's emotion mark
the end of our child-parent life.*

None of us can return home.

The childhood gift of "home" has been given and is carried within me.
I can handle the adult equivalent of skinned knees and playground bullies, for childhood rocking and safe refuge are a part of me. My parents'
love holds me still, for love is not bound by the walls of a house or a time
in space. It stretches through time and distance when we are apart.

The love of my parents lets me glimpse a larger, sacred love that also
holds me fast in dark, scary places, celebrates joy-filled times, and gives
me courage to venture into the mystery of the unknown. Their home-
love gives me a taste of sacred home. And leaving my childhood home
arouses primal echoes of divine homesickness.

To leave home is to traverse a terrain of terrible, stark beauty. It is a
timeless journey through sacred gift and loss and new birth. Difficult
and wondrous blessings are given the traveler. There are gifts from the
losses. Our child-parent relationship had to end for me to understand
that I carry inside this love that never ends. I had to leave home to know
this love that never leaves me when I walk out the front door.

Spiritual Practice
WALKING MEDITATION

"I have arrived
I am home
in the here
in the now ..."

Buddhist monk and Nobel Peace Prize nominee Thich Nhat Hanh assures us that the seed of mindfulness is sowed within us, but we forget to water it.[4] Walking reminds us that we are wayfarers on a journey, "visitors" like the Polish Rabbi Hafez Hayyim. The repetitive movement awakens us to repeating patterns in our lives. Our bodies teach us how to move through recurring patterns like the incessant rhythm of gift and loss.

Walking meditation is not about arriving at a destination. It is walking purely for the sake of walking. Intentional focus on the movement occurring right now gently brings us to be attentive. We arrive here—we are home in this present moment.

- Choose a place to walk. You do not need a destination, just walk for the sake of walking. Begin with a calm, relaxed pace. Do not rush.
- With each step, let go of worries and concerns. As you become lighter, let your face relax and your lips open into the smallest hint of a smile. Let your feet gently touch the earth with each step.
- Breathe in, breathe out. Do not try to control your breaths or your steps, but simply notice the number of steps you take with each inhalation and each exhalation.
- Silently repeat a word with each step. If you take three steps breathing in, say three words like, "I have arrived," or three prayer words. If you take three steps

with exhalation, say three prayer words or words like, "I am home."

    🐦 Be aware of your breaths and movement as you come home to this present moment.

Exploring Deeper

The cadence of birth and loss underlies life. Its persistent beat sounds every day and invites us to be attentive to repeating road markers on this strangely beautiful journey. Awareness of our astonishing early gifts and losses can help us recognize the enduring pattern of similar gifts and losses in our adult years. We are always leaving home.

Going Home

Memories of childhood experiences are the foundations of our present self. These memories are a mix of personal and borrowed remembrances. We can vividly recall high-school experiences but only partially remember our elementary years, and have little to no conscious memory of our toddler years. But our family shares their memories of these gap times, helping us "remember" that which happened before we can remember.

Journey back through personal and borrowed memories of your growing-up years. You can walk through all the years or only some of them. Explore them in a way and at a depth that is comfortable for you. There will be memories of the astounding gifts of childhood that you eagerly embrace, as well as remembrances you'd love to forget, and some that you choose not to reenter. You may want to gather some old pictures or a childhood memento. You can reflect further on the following questions in a journal with words or art.

    🐦 Settle into a comfortable chair. Allow unhurried time to remember. Light a candle if you like.

    🐦 What is your earliest memory?

      ❥ Can you tell any stories about your birth or early years? What do they say about you and about the family in which you were raised?

      ❥ Can you describe your childhood home so that others could picture it in their minds? What thoughts or feelings arise when you imaginatively walk through the front door of that home?

      ❥ What do you remember about your parents? How would you describe them? Who were your friends, other significant adults? Did you have a pet? If you were to imaginatively meet these people again, what thoughts or emotions might surface?

      ❥ Who loved you? How did you know—how did love manifest itself? What did it feel like to be loved? Do you yearn for that kind of love?

      ❥ Whom did you love?

Observing Other Leave-Takings

We have many second chances to reflect on the long process of growing up. Watching children around us through adult eyes, we can gain mature insights and new understanding of this experience. We may find it also prompts more of our own memories, and leads to deeper recollection and reflection upon our experiences.

      ❥ Be attentive to the ongoing cycle of gift and loss as it unfolds in children's experiences around you. What previously essential gifts are being outgrown? How is their loss difficult? What new gifts come from their loss?

      ❥ The following are some examples of situations you may encounter:

          ∞ A toddler's wild exploration, then hasty retreat to the safety of his father at the park

          ∞ A mother walking her child to school

          ∞ A neighbor child at your door selling "school fundraiser" chocolate as her dad protectively watches from the sidewalk

      A bus of middle-school soccer players traveling to an
      away game

      Beautifully attired young people celebrating prom night
      in a restaurant

      Your local high-school graduation

Leaving Home

Our final walk out the door of our childhood home evokes mixed thoughts
and emotions. This leaving home strings together all our earlier leave-
takings like beads on a necklace. Reflect on these questions to help you
remember your successive leavings of home as you grew older.

      Do you remember times of leaving home? It could have been
the first day of school, an overnight visit, summer camp, or a
school trip. Maybe you packed a peanut butter and jelly
sandwich and tried running away from home?

      How did your final leaving home happen? Was it to a job
and your own apartment, to volunteer or military service, to
school? How did you prepare for the move? What did you
pack? What were your thoughts and feelings before and on
that day and in the days and weeks after?

      What are your thoughts and feelings as you remember these
times?

Grieving Our Losses and Receiving Our Gifts

Growing up, we continually let go of outgrown gifts as we turn and turn
again to claim the gift of who we will become.

    The conclusion to this exercise rests on your previous remembrance
of the gifts of childhood. This is an invitation to explore your crucial
outgrowing of home and attachments to people in their childhood
form, so you could mature into an adult. What were the critical losses
of each stage of your journey, and what new gifts came from letting
them go?

- Viewing your memories through adult eyes, what did you lose with each step into more independence? What was it like to let go?
- Can you name new, perhaps surprising gifts associated with each loss? Could these gifts have been received without experiencing the associated loss?
- Where did you journey through terrain of terrible stark beauty—sacred ground which bestowed difficult and wondrous gifts of blessing?
- What gifts from childhood do you carry within you? What gifts have you physically let go, yet retained their blessing deep inside? This could be like carrying a parent's love deep within you after you leave home.
- What might this say about the sacred gift of birthright love?

Pray

You hover over the deep of each
not-yet moment,
You breathe me to life.

Thank you for home-places
of nourishment and growth.
May the fullness of their blessing
soak deep within.

Help me mourn
these passing gifts,
to let go even those I wish
to painfully hold on to,
and receive your Spirit's breath
moving over the water
creating gift and life anew.
Amen

Awakening: Patterns of Gift and Loss

3

The sun rises and the sun goes down, and
   hurries to the place where it rises.
The wind blows to the south, and goes round to
   the north;
round and round goes the wind, and on its
   circuits the wind returns.
All streams run to the sea, but the sea is not full;
to the place where the streams flow, there they
   continue to flow.

Ecclesiastes 1:5–7

Every moment bestows presents upon us as surely as snowflakes fall earthward and sun lights their crystals into fiery brilliance. And each moment brings the passing of gifts from our lives as inevitably as children grow up and leave home. We swim in a veritable river of gift and loss. And like fish, we are usually unaware of the water.

Awareness of this stream of gift flowing into loss flowing into gift is an incomparable teacher. We can awaken with wide-eyed wonder to the gifts that saturate our days. We smell the earthy moistness of rain as drops splat on stone, ping on windows, pulse a drowsy rhythm on the roof, and cool our upturned face. Our lips feel the fuzzy outside of a peach as we bite into the soft flesh and sweetness fills our mouth. We inhale a strawberry's fragrance, opening up memories of insects humming in Grandma's garden as our small sticky fingers pushed strawberry after strawberry into our overfull mouth. Amazed, we receive life's gifts in the fullness of all their colors, smells, textures, sounds, and tastes.

We also become attentive to the astounding flow of loss through our days. So many of life's presents have expiration dates. We're continually surprised by this until we awaken to the endless stream of loss. We outgrow vital, life-bestowing gifts as we mature. When their blessing has been fully given, it is ours to let them go in order to receive the gift of our future life. Even as we let go of these losses, new gifts of this present moment are being given.

But we also lose gifts we have not outgrown. Like the sun's daily arc of light moving across the landscape, the moment of their presence in our lives passes. Such losses of small gifts may go unnoticed. But the anguished losses of the loves of our lives overwhelm us, and we must fully walk through mourning them.

ADAM'S VISIT

In the desert silence, his car tires crunch the snow. I pull open Casa del Sol's heavy wood door with the red chili pepper wreath and lean against it as he parks. I'm delighted he's detouring to Ghost Ranch to visit me in the New Mexico desert, but I want him to start home with enough time to cross the high mountain passes in daylight. He can only stay an hour.

We hug in the bright sun. I can hardly believe he's here, standing in the courtyard of this adobe retreat house in the cirque of desert sandstone cliffs. We talk with lighthearted pleasure as I bask in this gift of his presence. An hour passes quickly. Leaving lunch dishes in the sink, he gives me a ride back to the ranch's main campus. Elated by his company, I say an upbeat good-bye and give him one last hug. As his dusty blue car disappears down the ranch road, tears unexpectedly sting my eyes and I feel a powerful wrenching. I'm taken aback at the intensity of my feelings. Resolutely turning, I brush away the tears and go inside to work.

Later, I walk the two miles back to Casa del Sol as sunlight dances on snow crystals. With my movement, ever-changing crystals are set alight by the sun until the entire desert floor is afire with dazzling brilliance.

Lifting the string latch on the chili pepper door, I walk into the kitchen to make tea. Our lunch dishes are in the sink and our benches are pushed away just as we left them. Adam's presence seems so close. I stand with one foot in the still-fresh experience of his visit, and the other foot in the reality of its loss. The pivotal moment of our leave-taking is so close that I can almost touch it. Now, I fully feel the loss. There's an ache deep inside and tears form again. This time I let them run down my cheeks.

I remember another good-bye and farewell hug and another moment watching Adam drive away in the same blue car, when he left home for his freshman year at a distant college. The emotions are still strong and fresh from this earlier leave-taking.

Now I understand. My hour with Adam was a gift that shines as bright as the sun on the snow. But my extraordinary sadness is not for the passing of that hour, but for a more profound loss and my not-yet-finished mourning of our three sons leaving home and the passing of our time as a family.

My heart—a mother's heart—yearns for those messy, chaotic, astonishing family days when the boys were young. The depth of my grief is tied to the wonder of the gifts I've lost—the three little boys I've watched grow into fascinating, delightfully quirky adults.

It's like wanting to hold the desert sunlight on a precise patch of snow crystals. I want to clutch one particular moment of breathtaking brilliance and not let it go. But there is nothing I can do. Even if I stand in the same spot, the turning of the earth alone will change the sparkling patterns.

The day after Adam's visit, the deep ache of loss returns as I put our washed lunch dishes away. I pull open the wooden door and walk to the base of the sandstone cliffs. A rock medicine wheel is laid in the desert floor. Holding open my hands, I offer prayer in the four directions for the remarkable gifts of our sons. Kneeling, I offer them to the sparkling snow-earth. And standing with arms outstretched, I offer them to the turquoise sky. The wind freezes my bare hands as it takes my thanksgiving for the gifts, and my pain at their loss, and lofts them high into the air.

Everyday Gifts

Adam's visit was a present wrapped in shiny paper, tied with a ribbon, and labeled "Mom." When life's presents are so obvious, it's easy to receive them fully, celebrate them with joy, and offer a prayer of gratitude.

But life's ordinary gifts are a little trickier to recognize and celebrate. Most importantly, we must be aware of them. Too easily, we competently navigate each day's twists and turns without noticing the terrain through which we pass as we miss the wonder of the day. But when we're attentive, we begin to see gifts in little moments and small details. Savoring each gift, we can turn it over and over to let its blessings fall upon us. Gratitude for the day's presents grows within us, and we say thank you more often.

My celebration of Adam's gift of a visit began with his unexpected phone call from Albuquerque—a conversation easily identified as a present and opened with delight. Even better was learning that he could take a detour to stop by Ghost Ranch for lunch. So I began to unwrap his gift even before he arrived. As I anticipated his visit, I sampled a little of the experience beforehand, tasting its joy in advance.

But I miss a lot of life's presents. How many gifts do I fail to see in an ordinary day?

One fall, my husband planted daffodils in the woods by our home, scattering the bulbs among pine, fir, and cedar. Winter lasts half the year in our mountains, so when spring finally arrives, water-soaked islands of brown forest floor emerge from snow on south-facing slopes and near the warmth of boulders. The next spring, I walked down the winding snow path, absorbed in my thoughts, and missed the tiny green daffodil blades poking up through the forest duff; I failed to celebrate this gift of spring's new life. Only days later, when the swelling at the top of the green shoots erupted into brilliant yellow, did I finally see.

There are so many ways *not* to see.

We miss gifts when we are preoccupied, asleep to the present moment. When we regret the past or fret about the future, we are absent to this moment and its overflowing gifts.

We readily overlook everyday presents that are tiny, so little that they do not register on our consciousness. Small pleasures surround us to be savored in all their richness, if only we see them. We also fail to notice gifts that arrive looking like ordinary pebbles strewn along our day's path. Dismissing them as commonplace rocks, we walk briskly over them and never suspect their treasure. And we choose not to see some of life's packages that come disguised in unpleasant wrappings. We quickly look the other way from them because we're anxious about what they might bring.

> *The old nun sits, silent and unmoving in morning's light. How many mornings has she received in her years? She watches. Light filtered through chestnut leaves falls on the wet grass. Dew reflects the light. A bird pecks the dirt. A yellow school bus turns into the high school next door.*

∾

Students talk noisily and laugh as they get off the bus. Seniors drive in fast, braking hard to park their trucks as music surges out of their rolled-down windows. A late-arriving teacher grabs her briefcase and slams the car door as she hurries into the building. The school bell rings, shrill.

⁓

She sits motionless, alert, looking. A child's old wood wagon filled with dirt overflows with flowers and bees. Sun's light awakens colors in the rough-cut monastery granite, red brick, and the old wood doors. A breeze stirs her hair. Coffee's dark aroma, pungent from the open refectory window, mingles with flower scent. A slow-crawling beetle navigates sidewalk cracks.

⁓

Trucks and cars pass quickly on the road to Cottonwood, their drivers looking straight ahead into the day's waiting tasks. A repair truck crunches up the gravel drive. The driver parks as he talks loudly on his cell phone while a talk show plays on his cab radio.

⁓

The bell high in St. Gertrude's tower rings its measured tone for morning prayers. She gets up.

Early light casts leaf shadows and shines in drops of dew each summer morning. The wonder of bird, bee, and beetle is an everyday present. Tantalizing coffee aroma, flowers' sweetness, and warm breeze are but a few ordinary, extraordinary gifts of daybreak, given in the space of a few minutes.

The nun is fully awake and attentive to the moment. With open hands, she receives the marvel of morning's light, water, creature, scent, and warm air.

How many gifts pass by us unnoticed? How often are we focused on our tasks like the students, the drivers on the road, and the repairman? When are we still? When do we stop to look in awed amazement?

We can cultivate awareness of the astounding gifts each minute brings to us. Rather than rushing through the day preoccupied and distracted, we can stop. Eyes and ears open, our senses awake to what unfolds in each instant. We can mindfully unwrap the countless gifts as their blessings soak deep into us.

Like a toddler looking at her first snow, we can stand astonished at the threshold of each day. Colors, sounds, smells, and tastes startle us with their vividness. Looking into the eyes of others, we awake to our deep connection and shared experiences of joy and pain. God gently breathes out and a wind sweeps over the waters. We begin to accept the sacred gift given so many years ago—the gift of being alive.

Our pilgrimage through life traverses beautiful and sometimes frightening terrain of gift and loss. But the life-giving rain of gift falls upon us even in the dry landscape of loss. Awake to the plethora of gifts, we are eventually led to awareness of the giver. While it seems we journey far from home, we become mindful of curious, ever-present provisions for us even in the desert of life-altering loss.

Everyday Losses

When we are attentive, we notice how many gifts of the moment are given only briefly. The movement from morning into day is an astonishing tidal flow of gifts coming and receding to make way for new gifts to be given. Early morning birdsong, dawn's impossible pink clouds, and first-light on dew-soaked grass—these are fleeting presents of the moment that pass almost as soon as they are given. Noticing them, we begin to awaken to the patterns and flow of this overarching stream of loss.

How do we respond to this unceasing rhythm? Our response to daily small losses can be a compelling teacher and a source of wisdom food to sustain us on journeys through our larger losses.

I'm writing this in late April. Friends from Texas and New Mexico, Florida and Maryland write to me of spring's glorious warmth, of grass greening and the explosion of flowers. They are giddy with an exuberant surge of energy and well-being. But in my Idaho mountains, large snowflakes fall steadily and abundantly as they have every day this week. Our house was fifty-nine degrees inside this morning, so a wood stove fire now provides our "spring" warmth. Coyotes and moose leave tracks in the many feet of snow outside while pine and fir trees are heavily laden.

Holding my friends' experiences of "spring" side by side with my own makes me smile, tempting me into a wistful yearning for warmth and budding new life during our mountain Aprils. But those of us who live here learn to accept our seasons. A humble posture of acceptance lets us hold our recurring loss of early spring very loosely. My husband merely grins and shakes his head at the snowfall. "It *is* beautiful, isn't it? Even in late April." The loss of spring's eminent arrival is not painful.

In a similar way, a multitude of small losses parade through all our weeks. Coined in the language of everyday circumstances, we often barely notice these losses as they flow quietly through our lives.

- Our freeway exit is temporarily closed for repairs. Without thinking about it, we take the next exit and wind our way back through town.
- We look for our favorite mechanical pencil before beginning a big project. Not finding it, we select a different pencil from the drawer and begin to work.
- A friend cannot make our scheduled lunch meeting today. We reschedule for next week, already planning on how we'll use this free time today.

For the most part, we hold our expectations regarding exits, pencils, and lunches lightly, so these little losses hardly create a ripple in our day; we calmly accept them as part of the great inhaling and exhaling of life. We merely alter our course and keep on walking without missing a step.

Little Losses, Big Reactions

But what about seemingly small losses that leave us sad and upset?

As April snow fell, a friend called. "I've had it with winter," she said, barely able to contain her emotion. "I'm beyond frustrated or sad. I'm depressed." Two days of sunshine had teased us earlier in the week, and she had luxuriated in a taste of spring while a crazy, childlike energy surged through her as she pored over garden catalogues and planned the summer's vegetable patch. But that morning, she shivered awake to a sky the color of slate, heavy snowfall, and tears.

We are vulnerable creatures living in a cosmos we cannot control. Unpredictable changes can bring us face to face with our defenselessness and threaten our shaky feelings of well-being. Our sense of self and our very welfare are often attached to our desires or expectations. Like a child clutching his beloved baby blanket, we clasp those expectations as tightly as a lifeline in a volatile sea.

Suddenly we care greatly about seemingly insignificant losses. If we're late for an important occasion, being detoured to a different freeway exit threatens our well-being. Desperate for our friend's advice over a difficult decision, we'll beg her to not cancel our lunch meeting. Hungering for spring's budding promise and summer's lazy glory, my friend gazes upon falling snow through her desire for sun, warmth, and sprouting garden plants and experiences tear-filled loss.

When we lose that to which we are closely attached, powerful thoughts and feelings flood us. Our angst and fear rests upon how closely our sense of self and wellness is tied to what we've lost. Seemingly small losses are no longer insignificant, but are wrested from our tightly clenched hands. They cause us a remarkable amount of unanticipated pain.

Uncovering Hidden Losses

There are other reasons why seemingly insignificant, everyday losses trigger surprisingly strong emotions. Minor events like a canceled appointment or a difference in opinion usually prompt easy adjustments.

Yet such losses can also evoke startling thoughts and strong emotions that arise from a hidden place and overwhelm us.

The intensity of my emotion when Adam left Ghost Ranch was bewildering and out of proportion to the passing of our time together. Later I realized my sadness did not really stem from the end of his visit, but from subterranean emotions that belonged to concealed, very significant losses in the past. Important losses can lurk underneath seemingly small losses. When minor losses cause unexplained pain, exploring the terrain beneath them can reveal larger losses that may not yet have been fully grieved.

Lilly shows up unexpectedly at my office. A professional woman, she's clearly anxious and upset. "I don't know what's happening," she confesses. The dentist's office called while she was en route to cancel her routine checkup this morning. Lilly was suddenly angry. She pounded the steering wheel and cried. Astounded by the power of her feelings, she didn't return to work but drove around and finally showed up here.

Words spill out at random. She's anxious at work. In a position for which she isn't specifically trained, she always feels unqualified and works long hours to compensate. She's uneasy about having missed an important meeting today to keep this dental appointment. Plus she's leaving next week for a month-long business trip to an isolated area in another country. Though she tells herself to stop worrying, and though she's learned all she can about her destination and her job, she has this odd nagging ache in the left side of her jaw. She starts crying. Last month she read about a traveler nearly dying from an untreated dental infection.

Why are such powerful emotions triggered by the minor inconvenience of a rescheduled checkup?

A cascading series of submerged losses hide beneath the cancellation. Already uncertain and insecure, Lilly has lost the assurance of attending an important meeting for an appointment that never even happened! Every day, she lives with the lack of confidence that she can do her job. Now the possible loss of her health looms large with the upcoming international trip.

Underlying the specifics of these losses is the ever-present, potent undercurrent of Lilly's vulnerability. The appointment's cancellation triggers a deep, unnamed fear of losing her tenuous sense of safety and security in life.

> *Gregor shows up precisely on time and briskly opens the council meeting. Pulling out notes, he outlines the current funding shortfall and offers a succinct analysis of the council's budget-cutting responses in the past. Passing out charts proposing similar measures, he recommends a quick vote so everyone can go home.*
>
> *But a new council member asks about alternative funding options, and another member recalls an innovative grant a neighboring town obtained. Discussion ensues as people think out loud and ask more questions. Gregor, obviously impatient, looks at his watch and shuffles his notes.*
>
> *The council spends an hour exploring alternate ways to address the budget problems as Gregor's face tightens and his posture becomes stiff. Finally, the group decides to delay a decision pending further research. Gregor casts the one dissenting vote, leaves the room in a huff, and slams the door behind him.*

Why has this hour of creative problem solving left Gregor infuriated? "I promised my wife I'd be home that evening," Gregor explains. "I've worked so many late nights. She was cooking my favorite dinner." He wonders if it is time for him to step down from the council. He had assumed the council would support his plan, since they'd always bowed to his considerable experience. But now, with the comfort of known ways in jeopardy, Gregor isn't sure he can lead them down untried paths.

Gregor has lost some fiercely grasped expectations. Besides an evening at home, he lost the council's affirmation of his years of experience. By not accepting his plan, Gregor lost his self-identity as a leader. The intensity of his emotions reflects the depth of his underlying losses and the strong grip with which he holds them.

Weaving throughout these narratives of hidden loss is the loss of a more primal yearning for some control over our safety and well-being. Lilly is anxious and unsure of herself and lives closest to the edge. Gregor works hard to maintain a tight sense of control and expects to influence the outcome of events he is involved in.

When circumstances beyond our control crash into our awareness, we confront the dreaded reality that we are not in charge of life. Awareness of loss on such a primal level as our desire for safety and to influence outcomes is foundation-shaking. When we are attentive, the loss of our illusion of control and the deep, unconscious fear it evokes underlies our pain-filled losses.

When the undercurrent of hidden loss catches us in its undertow, seemingly simple losses loom large and trigger unexpected emotions that can disrupt our lives and challenge our identity. But hidden losses can also be gifts. Consider this: the depth of our pain of loss is also the measure of our investment in what we've lost. Hidden losses can be the gift of opportunity to explore our fear-filled attachment to security, our continuing sense of vulnerability, our too-strong attachment to reputation and the affirmation of others, or our own need to control. And sometimes, as with Adam's visit, concealed losses unearth the depth and brilliance of the hidden treasure of a great love. Only a deep, immeasurable love could trigger such immeasurable feelings of loss when he leaves.

Spiritual Practice
EXAMEN

From the sixteenth century comes the spiritual exercise of *examen*, developed by St. Ignatius of Loyola. The prayer of *examen* invites us to explore patterns of gift and loss in our lives. This is a practice of looking back at our day, seeing ourselves as we moved through the day, and seeking the face of God, which we may have missed. Intended as an examination of conscience, we can engage the spirit of this traditional spiritual practice as a modern opportunity to mine our day for patterns of gifts and losses.

- Find a comfortable position in a place where you won't be disturbed. Settle into the silence.
- When you are ready, recall your day. With love, begin in the morning. Remember small pleasures such as sunshine, a stranger's smile, the sweetness of an orange, a helpful conversation. The longer you sit with the events of the day, the more gifts you notice. Take each sacred gift and hold it, look at it, and accept it gratefully. Be aware of how full the day has been with gifts.
- What are your thoughts or feelings about these gifts? Can you easily receive them and let them go? Are there any that are particularly precious or important to you? Any to which you feel attached?
- Going back again to the morning, recall the losses of the day. Did these losses occur as part of the flow of the day? Were there losses so small or so ordinary that you didn't notice them? These might be losses such as misplacing your favorite socks or the dog getting sick on the carpet.
- What was your response to these small losses? Did they flow easily through the day or did they cause pain or discomfort? Did some arouse surprising emotions? What does your

response tell you? Are there any losses hidden underneath? What can you learn from uncovering these hidden losses?

&. Are there any gifts that have flowed from the losses? Do you notice any patterns?

&. Rest in this moment, alive and fully awake to it.

Exploring Deeper

When we're present to this moment—right now—we awaken to life's tidal flow of grandly magnificent and touchingly small gifts every day. We also become aware of loss as gifts continually ebb from our lives.

There are many ways to be asleep to this endlessly repeating pattern. We are preoccupied and absorbed with our tasks and agendas, or engrossed with reliving, rehearsing, or rewriting the past. We're immersed in dreaming, orchestrating, or worrying about the future. Engaged in our own internal dialogue, we live in a mind-created world of our own making. We are robbed of living in this present moment, of receiving and letting go of its gifts as they pass by us unnoticed.

There are ways to cultivate awareness and to practice a posture of attentiveness. Keep a notebook handy to jot down your responses to these reflections in words or art. You may also want to write your own prayer in the pages of your notebook.

Past and Future

&. Settle quietly into a space where you will not be interrupted.

&. Be aware of your surroundings, the visual details, sounds, and silence. Notice your thoughts. What do you think about:

&. When you first awake in the morning?

&. While getting ready for the day?

&. When eating breakfast?

&. During the day, do you find yourself in the past, reliving certain situations with all their emotions? Do you find yourself absorbed by worries or daydreams of the future?

- Do not judge your thoughts, just acknowledge their presence in your days. Are there any patterns to your thoughts?
- Let your thoughts go. Be in the silence.

Processing

To further explore these experiences, it is helpful, sometimes, to go beyond words.

- Gather some old magazines, newspapers, colored or printed paper.
- Cut or tear out pictures, words or letters, colors and designs.
- Make a collage of repeating patterns. These could represent patterns in your life—patterns of thought, patterns of gift and loss, patterns of being asleep and awake.
- Leave the collage in your quiet space, to pray with and ponder.

Pray

God is our refuge and our strength,
A very present help in trouble.
Therefore, we will not fear, though the earth
    should change,
though the mountains shake in the heart of
    the sea;
though its waters roar and foam,
though the mountains tremble with its tumult.
                    Psalm 46:1–3

Things and Places

Long ago you laid the foundation of the earth,
and the heavens are the work of your hands.
They will perish, but you endure;
they will all wear out like a garment.
You change them like clothing, and they pass away;
but you are the same, and your years have no end.

Psalm 102:25–27

They come and they go: the places and things that we imbue with meaning right from the start. From our favorite blankie that we brought from crib to preschool, to our childhood home or our first apartment, to our collection of records or favorite books, these bits of material or real estate or vinyl or paper speak to us of the love of our family, make up the soundtrack of our teen years, and influence the people we've become. They are tangible gifts we can walk inside, see, hear, touch, or hold. And their loss is just as stunning and tangible, too.

After all, the passing of time inevitably changes all material objects and spaces. Things we cherish age and wear out. Living spaces are outgrown. Even creation's spaces are continually remodeled by spring's raging creeks, summer's drought-fueled forest fires, earthquakes, and volcanic eruptions—even as new life surges into fresh places. Our stunning lack of control over time and nature helps us let these changes—

these losses—flow through our hands, sometimes easily and sometimes only with great difficulty.

But in the end, we must simply let them go.

CAMPING

My husband eyes the slope of the ground as our sons scramble for tent sites with more pine needles than tree roots. As a mountain family in the West, we camp a lot.

Our camp sprouts quickly on the forest floor with small, brightly colored tents stretched tightly between arching poles. A little back-country burner flames as our one cooking pot provides comfort in sequence: first a warm one-dish supper, then hot drinks, and finally boiling wash water for bowls and spoons. Some distance from camp, Graham throws a rope over a pine branch and hangs our food supply high above inquisitive bears. Sleep follows the setting of the sun.

We instinctively settle into this piece of forest to which we temporarily belong. How easily tent sites and cooking and eating areas are established. I become acquainted with my own personal sitting boulder and the bend of a cedar trunk that matches the curve of my back for morning prayers. Attachments happen innocently and in quickly deepening succession. Something inside me yearns to make a home in this forest space.

After gentle conversations, laughter at supper, and a frosty shared sunrise spent waiting for water to boil, this site is imbued with experiences of people I love. The gift of our moments together saturates this place in the time-out-of-time we spend here.

There's an ache of loss when we break camp. Sleeping bags compress into stuff sacks, tents collapse, and back-pack straps cinch tight. I silently say good-bye to the trees

and boulders, and to the depressions left in the pine nee-
dles by our tents. As a mother and grandmother, I recog-
nize a woman's nesting attachments. But I also often see
my husband or one of our sons thoughtfully look back
into the forest before they turn to leave, and nod as
Graham announces to the universe, "That was a fine
campsite."

Some people take stunning pictures and tour famous
places, but I remember campsites—not where they are
on a map but the feel of that tree trunk holding me, the
angle of a particularly accommodating sitting boulder, a
shared cup of tea in a cold morning's silence, supper's
conversation under a darkening sky, and a forest walk to
water.

Openhanded Losses

Camps, of course, are temporary spaces we intentionally inhabit for a short time and then leave. In the grand tradition of nomads, a tent's roots are no deeper than its eight-inch stakes. As I pound those stakes while setting up camp, I know they will be pulled up again very soon. But still, feelings of regret and sadness arise over our inevitable breaking of camp.

The flow of such losses begins early in life. Baby dangles a toy over the edge of his highchair and it falls from his hand. A toddler drops her cookie in the dirt. A preschool child can't find his favorite T-shirt, which he tearfully insists he *must* wear today. A five-year-old leaves her beloved stuffed bear on the airplane. We are first carried, then toddle, then run through myriad places in our early years: grocery store, library, grandparents' house, preschool, the local park. Many children live in several homes in different cities even before they start kindergarten.

By adulthood we're well acquainted with this steady stream of small losses of objects and spaces. In that perverse cosmic plot, the dryer eats one sock of our only black pair. A cereal bowl slips from our hands and shatters on the floor. The break room at work is moved to a new location around the corner. While we transiently regret the inconvenience of their loss, it's easy enough to let these places and things go.

Lovingly Held Losses

In contrast, some places and things are deeply cherished. We lovingly vest them with meaning far beyond their physical presence. It's often not a conscious process, but happens gradually and with great love over time. If we lose them, we can be overwhelmed by the depth and complexity of our feelings. Their loss is complicated, painful, and emotionally laden. But losses like these are also invitations to look deeper, to explore what lies beneath.

> *I reach into my coat pocket. My fingers do not feel the comforting soft wool of my old knit hat. I turn back to look in the truck, but it's not there, or on the winding path up to the house. I mentally retrace my steps and call the restaurant while my son goes back to walk the snowy street in town. There's no hat. My stomach is tight. The hat was knit nearly thirty years ago when we lived in Europe. For years after this loss, I will get the same tight feeling in the pit of my stomach each time I open the cupboard to get my gloves ... and hat.*

> *Pulling the worn folder from the top drawer of his chest, Ibrahim turns the papers over one by one. All his important documents are here—except for the certificate of citizenship required by his new employer. He goes through each paper, unable to believe it is missing. He can request a replacement copy, but nothing can replace the original certificate. It embodies the pain and risk of*

leaving his homeland and family, his struggle to learn a new language and navigate a new culture, his hard work at low-paying jobs without adequate food or warm clothing. No copy can replace the paper he received that day he raised his hand to become a citizen.

My hat is so much more than a hat. I have woven into each stitch memories of the previous thirty years. In old pictures, I wear the newly made hat while hiking in the Alps with my husband and as I hold our first-born in Germany. I wear it in the U.S. as our two sons play in Midwest snow while visiting grandparents. And there it is again as we hike in England with our three boys. Our children are now grown, and I am still wearing that hat. It has value beyond value, a potent icon of our family and friends in all the places we've lived throughout the years.

The well-fingered naturalization document is so much more than a piece of paper. For Ibrahim, it is permeated with the aching losses of leaving behind a family and a previous life. It represents a decade of struggle in a new country, and it is imbued with the emotions of that moment he is able to walk into his brand-new life as an equal citizen.

On the surface, a hat and a citizenship certificate are an article of clothing and a piece of paper. But when they are suffused with memories of loved people, cherished ideals, and hopes, they powerfully embody that which is intangible, treasured, and meaningful. They become, in a way, sacred, and their loss evokes strong emotions that go far beyond their material worth.

We also invest places with our experiences and memories. The loss or alteration of these spaces similarly calls forth powerful feelings within us.

Maria calls me at church first thing in the morning. Could I come to her apartment, right now?

The noisy off-loading of a crane awakened her. She now fearfully hides behind the curtain of her window. Outside, glass shatters and signs are torn from a block of well-worn shops. These stores across the street have been Maria's lifeline. With the help of her social worker, she is living alone for the first time in her life. But how will she survive now? Tears tumble down her cheeks as she worries about herself and mourns the loss of Kesha, Jeramy, and dear Evie, the store clerks who are like family to her.

The apartment and shops are far more than just an apartment or a block of aging stores. This apartment is where she is nourished with food and renewed by sleep. The shops furnish everything she needs to live within walking distance—groceries and daily necessities plus the kindness and caring of people who know her name. It all supports and affirms Maria's longed-desired experience of living on her own.

We revere places that sustain us physically, socially, and spiritually. The places where we love and are loved, where we face our challenges and hold others' hands through hard times are holy. In mutual caring and love, we duck beneath our apparent separateness to meet on a deeper level. In this human love, we glimpse a more profound divine love for which we yearn. We taste for a brief moment coming home to that sacred presence for which we long.

This longing for home in its deepest spiritual sense has been voiced throughout the ages. Exiled Hebrews in ancient Babylon mournfully lamented the loss of their human home and the seeming loss of their sacred home.

> By the rivers of Babylon—there we sat down and there we wept when we remembered Zion.
>
> *Psalm 137:1*

The loss of our human home or human love arouses a more primal anxiety and loss. Echoes of our foundational longing, a divine homesickness, awaken within us as we become aware how far our pilgrim's journey seems to take us from our sacred home.

This is painful, hard loss. Maria is not just losing an apartment, but a place she calls home that embodies her hard-won independence and was saturated with the care and love of others. Ibrahim has not merely lost a replaceable document, but a piece of paper vested with his years of hardship to achieve a cherished ideal. When we recognize the symbolism behind such things and places, it is easier to understand our struggle with their loss.

Symbols of Gift and Loss

When we infuse an object or place with memories of people or with our ideals, beliefs, or hopes, we grant those things and places the powerful status of symbols. A symbol is much larger than its physical existence; it points beyond itself to that which is beyond words.

A communally held symbol is a wedding ring. Why do we wear a wedding ring, or feel incompletely attired when we forget to slip it on? Why does losing our ring cause us such angst?

A wedding ring serves a practical function: It wordlessly communicates that we are neither looking for a life partner nor are available to become one. It lubricates a community's social machinery by announcing our unavailability and dispelling unwanted advances. In the swiftness of a glance, that little circle of gold conveys important messages on multiple levels.

But it's more than a facilitator of appropriate social relationships. For couples, the ring is a sign of their profound love, embodying their commitment to each other through joyous and difficult times. A wedding ring speaks in powerful symbol language, pointing beyond its material presence on a finger to that which is so profound as to be inexpressible.

The loss of anything invested with the power of symbol evokes the profound emotions of losing that which it represents. When a symbol whose value and message is held in common is lost, we all can understand the impact. But other objects invested with private symbolic meaning—like an old knit hat, a citizenship paper, or a block of shops—speak just as powerfully, though the shock of their loss may not be understandable to others. The strong symbolic meaning of the object or place is concealed within us, as is the effect of its loss.

Let's look again at the powerful emotions evoked by the loss of something that we have vested with strong symbol value.

Lost and Found

Remember the campsite that I left with an unexpected tug of loss? Looking back, I wonder about the meaning that I've invested in this bit of forest. What does it symbolize to me?

My sadness, I think, didn't really arise from leaving towering trees, mossy boulders, and fast-flowing stream—they were delightful, but the forest is filled with other delightful places. Rather, I think this camping space embodied treasured time with people I love. I'm sorrowful for the passing of our family time together, and only when I can name this hidden loss can I claim it, mourn it, and truly let it go.

When I untangle my feelings of loss and identify the things I actually mourn, I can also understand what I *haven't* lost. Our evening at this campsite has ended, but the underlying gift of family love continues. Understanding and accepting this, I can liberate this forest I transiently imbued with my experience of family and let it return to being a loosely held gift of creation. Saying thank you, I can turn toward the gifts of this new day and fully embrace its fresh possibilities. Free of sadness, I leave our camp to receive the beauty of today's hike and the surprise of our next camp, evening supper, and shared conversation. From a feeling of loss comes a deeper gift of recognizing and receiving the enduring love of family.

I know that I don't really own trees and boulders, streams and campsites. I can enjoy these splendid gifts of God's creation, but I don't posses them. Because they can never "belong" to me, it's easier to let them go.

But objects may be more ambiguous, particularly human-made objects. We may indeed feel we possess them, and that they will belong to us forever.

> *Jose has never worn a watch. When he wants to know the time, he reaches into his vest pocket and pulls out his gold-plated pocket watch. He briefly fingers the smooth coolness of the case. Flipping open the cover, he squints into the old-fashioned face. In his later years, it's become hard to distinguish the spidery numerals, but the thick black hands are easy enough to see against the ivory watch face. His father gave him this watch—how many years ago? He and this watch were together at his wedding, on each day of his working life, at the graduations of his children and grandchildren, and most recently at the funeral of his wife, Isabella. Returning after a long trip to see his first great-grandchild, Jose wearily walks through his front door and, falling into his favorite chair, automatically reaches into his vest pocket.*
>
> *It's empty.*

Infused as it is with his father's love and a life of memories, Jose's watch is priceless. The slight weight of it in his vest pocket brings close the felt presence of his father; its coolness reminds him of the faces of his loved ones. Each opening of the gold cover, every look at its beautiful face comforts Jose, embracing him with the warmth of his family's love.

When this watch disappears, what has Jose lost? Surely, he lost a precious gift to which he is intensely attached. This is an authentic, heartfelt loss. He has lost his timekeeper and his memory keeper. After spending a lifetime instinctively reaching for it, fingering its cool surface, the watch has become a part of him. For the remainder of his days,

Jose will never stop reaching into his vest pocket, will never stop mourning the loss of this watch beyond value.

But that which Jose holds most precious—his memories and his family's love—are not lost. He retains the profound gift of his father's love and presence in his life. He retains the sweetness of his years of marriage to Isabella, the love of his life. He retains the memories of the family they raised together, and he has the continuing love of his children, grandchildren, and new great-grandchild.

In a similar way, I lost neither the love nor the vivid memories of the previous thirty years when I lost my beloved knit hat. Ibrahim did not lose his ideals, beliefs, and hopes when his citizenship paper disappeared. Nor did he lose the gift of his current life, the result of his years of struggle. And Maria did not lose memories of a precious experience of love and her taste of independence even if she had to change apartments—she can recognize the same sweetness in the future.

Our ability to love people, creatures and creation, ideals and beliefs is a gift. The image of God gleams within us when we love, shining through in flashes of brilliance. Our propensity to imbue things and places as symbols of this love will leave us bereft with their loss. The intensity of our bereavement goes far deeper than the lost object or space. It reaches into the sacred place of love and into our first, before-memory experience of divine love. It harkens back to that primal longing for sacred love and oneness that we perceive we've also lost.

Sacred Things and Sacred Places

Distinct from the symbolic value that we give certain objects and spaces is their inherent sacredness as part of creation. From this perspective, it is only right that we venerate the things and places of our lives. After all, in the beginning of every thing and every place, God hovers over the darkness of what is not yet. Breathed, spoken, and evolved into being, creation emanates from God, and continues to emanate as the changing seasons quietly teach us that God's creating is dynamic and ongoing.

Ever varying, the cosmos dances in response to sacred wind incessantly sweeping over the waters.

Different traditions reverence certain places with special sacred significance. Judaism reverences the remaining west foundation wall of the Second Temple, Christianity venerates the Church of the Holy Sepulchur, Islam reverences the Kaaba in Mecca, Hinduism venerates the city Varanasi. Synagogues, churches, mosques, and temples are respected places where humankind awakens and is attentive to the sacred. Celtic Christians speak of "thin places" where the veil between heaven and earth softens and we perceive the sacred.

It is our privilege to reverence all of creation. Black lichens spotting white granite boulders and earth's damp-smelling humus are divine gifts. Our family's old blue stoneware from which we've eaten while sharing our daily stories for twenty-five years is hallowed. Kitchen utensils for preparing food, my grandmother's handmade quilt, and the prayer shawl knit for me by a friend are blessed. The shovel we use to dig the garden—and even stink bugs, ubiquitous wizards at infiltrating our mountain home every fall, are holy. The very stuff of daily life is created from divine wind rippling the waters. It's all sacred.

There is a shift in our lives when we approach the things and spaces in life reverently. Our posture changes in relationship to created things. Our deferential approach to created matter and surroundings gradually awakens us to the giver and to divine presence. A sense of gratitude for these gifts rises up from deep within us. Aware that they are gifts to everyone and every creature, we are able to hold them lightly. We understand they are not ours alone and that we do not possess them.

Our grateful reverencing of created objects and places also leads us into increased awareness of their loss flowing through our lives. But when we hold these gifts lightly, they flow through our fingers with a prayer of gratitude for their passing presence. When aware of the sacredness of all creation, we cradle things and places gently in our open hands. And we just as gently let them go, our hands remaining open to receive future sacred gifts.

Clenching Our Hands

As human beings, we walk a fine line between gratefully receiving material things and creation's spaces and wanting to possess and hold them forever. Objects and places can easily become such an integral part of our self that we assume we're entitled to them. It is the gift of our continual experience of loss of things and places that keeps us grounded in the truth that we neither own—nor are we entitled to own—the things of creation. With each letting go of something or somewhere, we are reminded of their impermanence. Their loss and the persistent flow of loss teaches us to keep our hands open.

We receive many delightful spaces and things. They come into our lives and we relish their presence. We may infuse them with memories and form attachments to them. When this happens, there may be a shift in our posture in relationship to these created objects and places. Imperceptibly, we begin to hold them tightly. Over time, we forget that neither creation nor the objects of life really belong to us.

This is a dangerous pivot-point away from a life-giving stance of deeply reverencing things and places, holding them lightly, gratefully receiving their blessing, and relinquishing them. Our gentle acceptance covertly turns into peril when we curl our fingers around these gifts and hold them forcefully in clenched hands. It is seductively easy to believe we "possess" and "own" them.

There is great risk here. We become possessed and controlled by the very things and places we covet. We succumb to siren songs. There's a sliver of dark truth in each of us, embodied by J.R.R. Tolkien's character Gollum in *The Lord of the Rings*. Once a graceful creature belonging to freely flowing river water, Gollum changes as he becomes obsessed with owning a ring he lost. Continually muttering to himself, he is possessed by "my precious, my precious" ring. "Where iss it, where iss it: my Precious, my Precious? It's ours, it is, and we wants it."[1]

In the end, the gleaming circle of gold for which he grasps so desperately destroys him.

Often, it is our deep-seated fears that provoke such acquisitive clutching of things or places. Within each of us is a strong desire for security, safety, comfort, food, and water. There are also yearnings for control—and even for power—in us all. When we're threatened with the loss of these things that we desire, fear pays us a thundering visit. Fear is the Gollum force that drives our hands to grasp and hold tightly to things and places.

These desires needn't be so sinister that we feel a need to speak in whispered tones about their presence in us. Woven into my swift settling into camp is surely an unspoken yearning for security and safety in the forest with food and water, the comfort of companionship, and sleeping-bag warmth. My favored path to the water, preferred sitting rock, and easily established patterns are intertwined with a primal desire for some sense of control amidst back-country wildness. Breaking camp also breaks open my temporarily established sense of safety, comfort, and control. My twinge of sadness is undoubtedly laced with a small dose of an ancient fear of losing safety and security, exposing me as the vulnerable creature I am.

The more tightly we grasp a place or a thing, the more powerful the flare of pain with its loss. It is relatively simple for me to let go of a one-night campsite with its attendant memories. It's a bit more difficult for me to let go of a hat that's accompanied me for three decades. Ibrahim experiences considerable pain in losing a citizenship paper that is the culmination of several decades of wrenching loss and transition. Maria is filled with fear at the loss of shops and people that are her lifeline to an independent existence. And anguish pervades Jose's loss of his beloved father's watch, which holds an entire lifetime of memories in these last years of his life.

Spiritual Practice
SAND MANDALA

A Tibetan Buddhist tradition is the ritual creation and destruction of intricate geometric designs (mandalas) made of colored grains of sand. Before construction begins, the large, complicated pattern is carefully drawn. A team of monks will work for several weeks to painstakingly place brightly colored sand grains on the drawn design.

After the ceremonial viewing is finished, the completed mandala is destroyed in an elaborate ritual. The grains of sand are released into a river or stream of running water and returned back to nature from whence they came. This practice involves a profound experience of letting go and an unforgettable reminder of the transitory nature of all material things.

- Go outside and look carefully at all that surrounds you. Be aware of its great gift.
- Reverently gather natural things—rocks, seeds, grasses, sand, flowers, twigs, leaves, pine needles. You may also use colored sand like the Tibetan monks.
- Take time over the next days to carefully place these natural objects in a pattern on a table, the floor, or a large poster board. You may draw an intricate pattern first or spontaneously arrange elements where they seem to fit over the next days. Take care and delight in the creating, giving thanks for the gifts of rock, sand, and living plants.
- Gratefully appreciate your completed design. Then let it go. Reverently collect all the things in the design and return them to the outside world.

Exploring Deeper

We often walk quickly through our days, concentrating on tasks and meetings. Frequently, we only notice our material world when we can't find an object or when something we need breaks.

- ❧ Look around the room in which you are sitting. Let your eyes rest one by one on the objects of your daily life. Acknowledge their gift and offer a prayer of thanks.
- ❧ Gratefully recall the activities that have taken place in the past in this room. Remember those things and the people involved, and think of the things that will continue to happen in this room.

Lovingly Held Things and Places

Our lives are usually blessed with a few objects that are of great importance to us. Their significance may have nothing to do with their usefulness or their material value.

- ❧ Remember a treasured gift given to you by a person you loved. It might be a special cup, a rock, a child's scribbles, something to wear, or a dried flower.
- ❧ Recall an object that represents a deeply held ideal or belief. It could be a religious symbol, a memento of an important occasion, or a certificate.
- ❧ Look at why you value these objects and put into words why they mean so much to you.
- ❧ How would you feel if you lost such an item or if it broke? Can you name what has been lost? Can you articulate what has not been lost?

We also imbue special places in our lives with great significance. Their importance to us is a measure of the magnitude and meaning of what happened there.

- Can you describe a place that has particular meaning for you? Why is it important?
- What are your thoughts and emotions when you visit this place, either through pictures, your imagination, or an actual return?
- What are your thoughts and feelings as this space changes over time?
- What have you lost? What have you not lost?

Unclenching Our Hands

- Settle into a comfortable place. Give yourself a fair amount of time. Recall this day's responsibilities and tasks that remain incomplete. Let each of them go one by one. They will wait for you.
- Remember one thing or one place that is a precious symbol to you of someone you love, a belief, or an ideal.
- If you are thinking of a meaningful thing, imagine holding the object. Appreciate the feel of it in your hand: its weight, shape, texture, color, uniqueness, beauty.
- If you are thinking of a significant place, see it in your mind, hear the surrounding sounds, feel the heat or cool of the air. Sit for awhile and appreciate the space.
- Recall the people, beliefs, or ideals that are symbolized by this object or place. Gently hold them separate from the symbol. Do you hold them loosely or tightly?
- Imagine holding them lightly in open hands, then visualize gently letting them go.

Pray

My fingers hold tight,
clasping what
I think is mine.

Why can't I let go
of what will change
anyway?

If I could reverence it all as sacred—
I'd know it never did
belong to me.
Amen

The Ebb and Flow
of Relationships

I am about to do a new thing; now it springs
forth, do you not perceive it?

Isaiah 43:19

Just because we've "grown up" doesn't mean we're finished creations. Sacred wind of new creation continues to blow through our adult lives as we persistently change and grow. We will walk through many personal seasons of spring and summer as well as autumn and winter periods. Lasting relationships that honor both people provide ample space for such enduring growth and stretching. Our persistent maturing stretches not just ourselves—it also stretches our relationships into new places.

We have tasted human love, and through this love we have glimpsed our birthright of sacred love. Such profound love enables us to risk continuing change—change in ourselves, in those we love, and in our relationships. Grounded in love, we are free to let go of outgrown ways of relating to let something new flower. This is the sacred ground of all healthy, lasting relationships as they transform to nourish us in fresh and surprising ways.

Earlier we explored how the astounding changes of our growing up required stretching and changing our relationships with our parents.

69

We let go of a lot, as did our parents, to enable the new, radically altered relationship between parent and adult child.

Let us now look at these parental losses to understand the essential losses that let long-term relationships continue to be life giving, whether between parents and adult children, spouses, or friends.

MOTHER OF THE GROOM

My black-suited eldest son walks toward me up the path. He's all grown up, finished with college. And yet, as I watch him come closer, I catch a glimpse of a kicking, wet, newborn Ian, howling in indignation at his birth. I see one-year-old Ian, screeching in delight and hanging on tight as we wild-dance to fierce music from the opera Carmen. *I briefly feel the curve of his four-year-old body against mine in the swinging chair, as we read book after book on a rainy afternoon. I hear his first-grade voice painstakingly sounding out "wah-hat" every time he sees the word "what." There he is climbing school-bus steps, and then behind the wheel of the car as we spend hours together before his driving test. Now, as he nears the end of the path, I see college-graduate Ian in cap and gown, just last month. He smiles at me, turns, and stands at my side.*

We wait. Gold threads on red brocade catch the light. Charity, in a formal Vietnamese wedding dress, starts up the path. I hear Tevye and Golde's voices from Fiddler on the Roof: *"Is this the little girl I carried? Is this the little boy at play? I don't remember growing older. When did they?"*

He repeats after me, his wedding vows.

"I, Ian, promise you, Charity, to be your loving and faithful husband."

Jagged snow peaks of the Canadian Rockies witness their promises. Towering pine and fir watch as they exchange rings. We all see them kiss. I pronounce them husband and wife. "Husband Ian" now joins "infant-toddler, elementary-school, college-graduate Ian" as we surround the couple with hugs and blessings.

The wonder and awe of a wedding is an astonishing celebration of bittersweet joy for parents. It marks the forever loss of our tender, intimate parent-child relationship and heralds the wondrous gift of our adult child's commitment to a new love. Weddings truly are laden with happiness and tears.

Years earlier, we brought home this new little being that turned our lives upside down. Nothing could have prepared us for this—neither sage advice from other parents nor our own months of anticipation and preparation. Gazing into this tiny face, we were astounded at his existence. The intensity of our love for this baby overwhelmed us. This was a unique love, the likes of which we'd never before known.

Equally overwhelming were the momentous life changes occasioned by the arrival of this child. We could not have understood this earlier. All the stories we'd heard about sleepless nights, marathon crying spells, and constant care could not prepare us.

Whether we give birth or adopt this little one, we enter the free fall of extraordinary loss of self that is required to parent a child.

There are clues, brief tastes, of this intense loss of self before baby comes home.

I'm ecstatic to be pregnant with Ian. I can live with the nausea—it won't last forever. And I'll navigate through the seductive siren song calling me to an afternoon nap—impossible with my full patient schedule at the clinic. By three in the afternoon, any horizontal surface lures me to rest.

But energy and appetite return in pregnancy's middle months, and this sweet little bump of a new being appears.

But the bump grows to alarming proportions in the last months. Alarmed, I survey my silhouette with dismay and foreboding. Whatever could God have been thinking? How can this elephant of a child (he weighed six pounds and a few ounces!) possibly be born? Maternity clothes grow tight, everything aches, and I know the location of every bathroom in a fifty-mile radius. I can't sleep comfortably, and my husband gives me a helpful push to get me out of bed. With this growing child on autopilot, the stunning lack of control over my body is the most obvious loss in pregnancy. But on the periphery hovers a vague loss of peace for both Gary and me, anxious about the unknown of impending birth.

Contractions begin quietly, but soon crescendo in relentless, ever-tightening circles. Waves of breathtaking pain parse the minutes and hours. Overwhelming all other reality, nothing else exists as the world collapses into the relentless rhythm of labor.

At some point in this time-out-of-time world, a primitive urge to push rises strong and compelling. Sleep-deprived and at the end of my reserves, every fiber in my body screams, "Push." But the nurses tell me to wait. With their encouragement, I take deep breaths and venture past my ability to cope. Gary and I wander far beyond the wilderness in those last hours of labor.

Parenthood: A Crash Course in Letting Go

Birth is a crash course in letting go. It is surrender of mind and body and spirit to something primal and cosmic, a fleeting glimpse into eternity. This is the unmistakable lesson that something in us must die for birth to happen. Loss is absolutely necessary for anything new to be born. The enormity of loss mirrors the magnitude of change occasioned by birth.

With birthing a baby , our desire for control, to avoid pain, and to sleep rather than drench ourselves in the sweaty work of this forever ordeal must face a death of sorts. And this is just the beginning.

Adoptive parents experience their own deaths and their own anxious loss of control. There are months or years of paperwork, interviews, and caseworker visits as they experience surrender of privacy. But just as hope starts to fade, the phone rings, and news of a baby often comes just hours or days ahead of time. What seemed an unending wait now takes an abrupt U-turn. A child! With this joyous-anxious news comes a last-minute burst of shopping for baby supplies and sometimes a nervous, excited airplane flight halfway around the world into another culture to meet their child for the first time. There's no going back.

No matter how baby arrives, when we step across the threshold to carry our new little one home, we walk through the front door into a forever-changed way of life. The child's demand on our lives is astounding. In the first hazy, sleep-deprived months, we lose any sense of control. The very fabric of our previous life, centered on work, our own needs—and even our whims—is turned upside down. We leave behind our former world of spontaneous, carefree activities to focus on loving and taking care of this child. We will never be the same again.

A love so tender and profound it stuns us will lead us through these losses and monumental changes. Once we finally let go of our previous life to take care of baby, we begin to delight in the intimacy of this new-found relationship. We relish time together as we gaze absolutely smitten into the beauty of our newborn's face, snuggle our one-year-old, cuddle and read to our toddler, or kick a soccer ball with our pre-schooler. Yet even as we experience these depths of love and settle into its constant demands, our child begins the long process of pulling away. Having lost so much to finally arrive at a degree of selflessness, the irony is that we will now mourn the inexorable loss of this closeness over the next decades as baby grows up.

First crawling, then walking, bicycling, and finally driving away—baby embarks on the long journey of stretching, diminishing, and finally severing childhood attachments to us. Even as we celebrate milestones of independence, we have been so radically changed by parenthood that we now also experience melancholy loss.

But parents want their children to develop into self-sufficient grownups with lives and relationships of their own, to be healthy and independent enough to leave home. Right?

Well, mostly right. We all know deep inside that our tender moments of closeness will pass. One day our child will leave home. But that's *years* in the future.

"Wasn't it yesterday when they were small?" asks Tevye in *Fiddler on the Roof*. It's a question all parents ask with a poignant mixture of wonder and loss. Our exquisite newborn develops into a combination of pure angel and real human being with problems and eccentricities. Yet, it is precisely our children's difficult habits that help us play the pivotal role of nurturing them and letting them go as mature adults.

Some children help their parents each step of the way toward letting them go. They perfect their difficult behavior in adolescence, sometimes peaking in the arduous last years of high school. Their efforts, vaguely reminiscent of a two-year-old's temper tantrums, pry open our parental hands a little more willingly—they have so outgrown our old relationship! When their last day at home finally dawns, parents can take a deep breath and wave good-bye with fewer tears and heartbreak than might have been.

We practice for our children's leaving home in a decades-long dance. Each stage of relationship with our growing child offers experience in letting go of what is outgrown to embrace a new way of relating. From letting our little one stay overnight with a friend, to spending after-school time with classmates, to driving a car, to staying out late—raising our children into adults persistently stretches and alters our relationship to give their emerging self space to grow and blossom.

There are, of course, other losses, as one of my patients painfully understands.

At a routine checkup, I talk with Akio about his elevated blood pressure. Sighing, he becomes visibly stressed about his son's departure for college next month. An engineer, Akio shakes his head about his son's art school tuition. "We can barely afford the payments," he frets. "And tell me, how will he ever make a living from art?"

Akio wonders how things would be different if his parents hadn't immigrated to this country when he was young. "Sometimes, the old ways are better," he says tersely. Akio was taught to listen to his parents, to respect their wishes. But his son, born and raised in America, thinks he can do whatever he wishes. "All he thinks about is art; he's been scribbling since he was a little kid, doodling in math class—math class, mind you, an important subject! He's still playing with clay and taking pottery classes." All these past years of tension now culminate in next month's trip to his son's new "art school."

Great Expectations: Our Children

We all share common expectations for our children. We teach them to look both ways before crossing the street, eat healthy food, not throw sand in the sandbox, learn their lessons at school, and obey the lifeguard. But we also have unique expectations that begin even before they are born. During pregnancy, we may construct a fantasy about our infant: she'll have Daddy's brown eyes, Mommy's curly hair, and from the way she's kicking, she'll be a great soccer player. When she turns out to be a totally different person, we quickly adjust our mental image to delight in this surprising baby just as she is. Loss of our expectations enables us to receive this wondrous gift in surprise wrappings.

"I can't wait to take her ice skating ... show him the art gallery ... bring her hiking ... introduce him to the garden ... teach her how to care for her own horse ..." We all want to share our favorite things in life with our offspring. But how quickly can we let go of our disappointment when they show no interest or aptitude for our passions? How graciously can we embrace the children we are given and enjoy their distinctive interests? We must continually shed our expectations to let our children grow into their unique, astonishing selves. Our explicit hopes and assumptions form the "above-water" part of the mammoth iceberg of our expectations.

But many of our unspoken dreams for them remain submerged, hidden even from our own consciousness.

Sitting on the park bench, Lani and I watch our kids play. Laughing, she tells me about their watercolor experience this morning. "Malia spreads huge patches of color all over the paper. Of course, she's very generous with the water and creates rainbow lakes that pool on the paper and run over the edge." Lani confesses to being impatient with Malia's "mess" of a painting. "What beautiful colors," Lani tells Malia as she quickly removes the sodden paper to the counter to dry.

But then her son Kai becomes interested in the paints. Lani watches, fascinated, as he also makes pools of color and shapes on the paper. "How beautiful," she tells Kai. She finds more paints and gives him a second sheet of paper.

Only later, when she sees the children's paintings drying, does Lani realize how differently she treated her two children. "All I saw was the mess of Malia's painting. I don't really expect anything to come from her playing with paint since neither her father nor I have artistic talent. But Kai made a similar mess, and I watched for the sheer surprise of possibly seeing unknown gifts unfold. Sometimes I'm a better parent to

my adopted children." Since Lani doesn't know Kai's
birth parents, she doesn't assume to know what Kai can
or can't do. He's free to pursue any interest and to follow
any direction through the open, untracked territory of
his future. But, she laments, "I've plenty of assumptions
about Malia, and I narrow her future because of it."

Lucky for us, our children stubbornly help us let go of our expectations. Tenaciously pursuing their own passions, they assist us to let them grow into their unique selves. From clothing styles, to hairdos, to piercings, to friends and interests, they assert their individuality. As parents, we are to hold them ever so lightly, providing love and space for them to blossom into themselves.

Great Expectations: Ourselves

But what about our own expectations as parents? At a childbirth class, Ahmed shared that he and his wife had watched a frazzled mother offer her child candy to quit whining about buying a toy at the store. Shaking his head, gazing at his wife's very pregnant belly, he said in a gentle voice, "I will never bribe our child."

Observing life's cafeteria of parenting styles, who hasn't watched a parent whose behavior we vow we'll *never* do ourselves? (This is much easier to do before we have children.) Offering a celebratory sticker to our two-year-old son after a successful potty trip, I also remember promising to not "bribe" my children. I quickly justify the sticker as "positive reinforcement."

When we look into the mirror each morning, we must acknowledge the loss of a glimpse of the ideal parent. Looking back at us instead is a quite acceptable parent. We have many days and moments of being loving parents who share that love with our child and address situations appropriately. But we also have occasions when we don't act out of our best selves and our love, when we are tired or short tempered, when our children drive us nuts. We're human just like our parents, and just like our children.

> *Ordering a CT scan for a little boy who fell at the play-ground, my colleague shakes his head. "Things like this make me an anxious wreck when I take my daughter to the playground. I follow her, shadowing every climb and walk across the balance beam, ready to catch her if she trips." He's seen nearly every type of playground injury in his emergency department work. Every time he looks at a playground, he sees an accident waiting to happen. "I either need to work somewhere else, or her mother needs to be the playground parent."*

From the moment our children are born, it's our natural instinct to shield them from harm. And yet, life happens. One-year-olds fall off couches, first graders tumble from climbing gyms, teenagers take risks. We do not control all the outcomes; some situations are beyond our influence.

Only love—that bottomless love we felt with their first kick—can sustain a relationship with our children that will change more than any other relationship through the years. Only love—that infinite love we felt with our first look into their new faces—can help us grow into the radically altered relationship that we'll need to develop with our adult children.

The gradual loss of our earliest tender parenting and our explicit and hidden expectations for our children and our self is essential. But we are often startled by the intensity of these losses. We have lost this child who rocked our lives with his arrival and immense needs, who then persist-ently and inevitably left us in degrees. We were emptied of our self by his coming, and now we're emptied of intimate, sweet closeness by his leaving.

The magnitude of our love for the gift of this child births the enor-mity of our loss. And yet, this great love also enables us to let go. Love guides us through the loss, to embrace the gift of our adult son or daughter in a transformed relationship.

The time may come when we see our child wed another. Something irretrievable shifts in the universe. With a love that brings tears to mother's eyes and a lump to father's throat, a love that pulls us into the very depths of spirit-inspired love—we love them enough to let them go. In an act of astonishing grace, in a gesture surely in the image of God-love, parents freely "give away" their children on the momentous day that they are married.

Evolution of Love and Loss

Maybe you met your partner in school and he is the love of your youth. Or perhaps you came together after other loves and other experiences. Maybe your love is the sweet present of your golden years, when you thought widowhood or age had brought an end to such pleasure.

The couples I've married are utterly sincere when they promise themselves to each other. They repeat words imbued with ageless wisdom.

> *I promise to be loving and faithful,*
> *"in times of plenty and in want;*
> *in joy and in sorrow;*
> *in sickness and in health;*
> *as long as we both shall live."*[1]

These words carry profound insight for all long-term relationships. Unflinchingly honest, they tell us that everything will change—ourselves as individuals, our relationship, and the circumstances of our lives! The words warn us unequivocally that there will be loss, for that is the cost of our love. But from these losses, a transforming relationship can continue to emerge, phoenixlike, one that is much wiser, deeper, and often delightfully surprising.

As I watch people in many different types of long-term relationships, I frequently hear the words of this marriage vow echo as their wisdom rings true. There are similar dynamics of loss and growth in any lengthy relationship, whether between family members, among good friends, or within communities. We can explore the pattern of these losses in any committed relationship by looking at a lifelong marriage.

> *I soon get used to the rhythmic whish-whish of Seamus's oxygen as he and his lifetime sweetheart, Kate, reminisce about their courtship. "In a grove of trees at the edge of town," Seamus says, "there's a heart carved into the bark of an old tree. We put our names in that heart almost six decades ago. The tree's grown, but if you know where to look, you can still see what remains of that heart and our names."*
>
> *"Remember, my parents didn't want us to marry," Kate kids Seamus. "They thought you weren't good enough for me."*
>
> *A smiling Seamus replies, "Clearly, they were right." But finally giving in to headstrong desires of youth, Kate and Seamus promised each other in a small ceremony to be "loving and faithful."*
>
> *Those first years were good; they both grin as they reminisce. "Remember that miniscule apartment over the hardware store? Never sure we'd make the next rent payment, we had just enough hand-me-down plates for us and one guest," recalls Kate.*
>
> *"But we were together. And that was everything," Seamus adds. Looking back, those early times of barely getting by seem like times of plenty indeed.*

But honeymoons don't last forever. The initial attraction doesn't maintain its intensity. Early years of living so closely together, the weight of new responsibilities, the stress of worries all bring people to see each other in a new way. Those endearing quirks can rapidly grow into irritating annoyances.

> *"You were messy,"* Kate says. *"How could that tall Seamus-charmer who wooed me with flowers and gifts turn into someone who dropped his dirty clothes all over our apartment and dripped all over the bathroom? Plus you snored, horribly."*
>
> *"Dripped?"* Seamus asks. *"I dripped? Ah, but you were a terror in the mornings. How could that Kate-beauty who mesmerized me with her carefree spirit be such an angry growler? No man or beast should cross your path until at least midmorning."*

Kate and Seamus do not talk about their tearful and angry arguments. They do not mention visits to their pastor, where they sat on the couch as far apart from each other as possible, while Seamus nervously twisted his wedding ring around and around as a tense Kate sat bolt upright. At those meetings, one sentence could flare their anger, and pent-up emotions could erupt in a torrent of hurtful words.

Our romantic visions of a perfect marriage with an ideal partner shatter into pieces after the honeymoon. The shards of our early fantasies litter the floor. We are bewildered, frustrated, and angry.

Amidst the rubble of our dream marriage, we also have the audacity to hold up a mirror to each other and demand that our partner acknowledge his or her imperfection. We wrestle with the loss of our carefully constructed self-image, as we mourn the loss of our romanticized relationship with a formerly flawless spouse. These losses are painful, deep, and far-reaching, truly "times of want."

If both people in a relationship are willing, though, we can claim a hard-won gift of a new reality. As illusions about ourselves, our spouse, and our marriage are torn open, we unwrap a sobering, costly gift born of loss. Entering into self-stripping honesty, we begin to see the actual people who inhabit this relationship. There is a shift, a radical change in our self and in our marriage. We can now look at ourselves, our loved one, and our relationship with a level gaze—and hopefully still say, "I do."

> *Kate reminisces, "Remember those times at the park? We'd pack cheese and bologna sandwiches to eat under our tree, and our daughter took her first steps in its shade. So much good came our way. You went back to school, found a good job. We finally moved into a place bigger than a closet."*
>
> *Seamus looks at Kate. "You still mesmerize me," he says.*
> *"And you're still a charming devil," Kate replies.*

Kate and Seamus have the costly gift of a mature, honest relationship, given only through the painful loss of their illusions about themselves, each other, and their marriage. Only through the eyes of mature love can they see the beauty and gift of the other as well as their difficult characteristics.

And only maturity can let them look in the mirror of their finally large enough house and acknowledge their gifts and their difficult traits. The gift of their grown-up relationship only comes from the graceful, persistent loss of that which they've outgrown, as they and their relationship changes and grows. They hold one another loosely, letting each other develop and transform throughout their life. Having navigated their losses, they can accept the priceless gift of this relationship and all their "times of joy."

Seasons of Friendship

A person's family comes as a package deal, and those people know pretty much everything about us. They changed our diapers, cheered our first steps, delighted in our gap-toothed first-grade picture, tolerated our middle-school angst, and attended our high-school graduation. Our favorite aunt or uncle gave us that totally impractical present we secretly always wanted. Our grandparents, siblings, and cousins witness our years of radical change. Fiercely committed to us, they let our relationship transform as we grow.

Trusted friends may do everything our family does—grow with us over time, accompany us through difficult periods, celebrate our joys. But good friends love us and we love them because we freely choose to do so. They are faithfully present for us, without any familial obligations. In fact, if the family we didn't choose turns out to be unsupportive or unloving, our close friends may assume that nurturing role.

Most ongoing friendships begin in our adult years. Something draws us together—shared interests may put us in close, frequent proximity, or our personalities just seem to fit. Maybe we're intrigued by our differences, fascinated by another's distinctive gifts and life, so enticingly unlike ours. Whatever attracts us, we become and remain friends because each of us desires to be friends. We voluntarily commit to our relationship.

But commitment to another person always entails loss. Saying yes to one person means we must say no to others. Often our "no" is concealed, even from us. To form and nurture a friendship requires a subtle, sometimes hidden turning from other pursuits and people—there are, after all, only so many hours in the day, and we must decide, either consciously or subconsciously, how to spend them. Because of this commitment, we may have many acquaintances, but only a few good friends.

Our journey into long-term friendship shares many characteristics with the deepening of any lengthy relationship. There is an initial, golden "honeymoon" period of pure enjoyment in being together. As the relationship develops, we savor our friend's unique gifts. And inevitably, as we begin to notice our friend's weaknesses and difficult characteristics, we start to lose our illusion of the person we imagined, or wished, or needed our friend to be. As the friendship continues, we learn to let go of unreasonable expectations of our relationship and to accept our friend and our relationship "as is."

There will also be continuing losses. Just like our children, parents, spouses, and ourselves, our friends continue to mature and change over time, and like the other important relationships in our lives, we need to hold our friendships loosely. A healthy friendship is an organic, flexible give-and-take that changes throughout time. Jean Vanier, founder of L'Arche communities where people with and without disabilities share their lives in familylike homes, beautifully describes a posture of gently holding another. He teaches us to have lightly cupped hands as if holding a small bird: not flat so that the bird falls out, and not grasping so tightly that the bird is crushed and dies. A lightly cupped hand is the space where growth of the other, and our relationship, can occur.

We will lose something even more valuable in a long-term relationship. As part of giving and receiving, we gradually drop our masks, becoming less guarded about our inner selves. Sharing hopes and dreams, we also share disappointments, hurts, and our most secret wounded places. Eventually, in the fullness of deep friendship, we reveal our weaknesses, blind spots, and frailties. We let go of our pretenses, losing some of the illusions we carry about ourselves.

This sharing from our most vulnerable center can be messy and scary. We loosen our suspicions and need for security, trusting the other enough to risk intimacy. We let down our masks and crack our protective outer shell to reveal our tender places. Then we wait to see if that trust is justified. If we are both willing to walk through the difficult place of receiving and revealing weaknesses, limitations, and rough edges, our friendship can develop deep roots that hold us together beyond a surface sharing of common experiences or interests.

As years pass, we increasingly know each other well as we write a common history together. Our friendship matures into a love that desires our friend's well-being and wishes to be present for our friend's needs. Together, we continually learn the dance step of bending gracefully to let go of that which is old to accept the gift of new possibilities.

Our friendship is a gift in which we repeatedly choose to offer and receive life. Such relationships can last a lifetime.

Love: The Underlying Thread

It is love that brings us into relationship and love that sustains us through these losses. Love guides us in the painful letting go of illusions about ourselves and about the other with whom we have relationship. Love enables us to let go of romantic fantasies about our relationship itself. And finally, love lets us hold the other and our relationship in gently cupped hands, gracefully letting the loss of outgrown ways flow through our fingers. We can then let the other and our self grow and change, embracing and accepting our new ways of relating.

Meeting each other in the depth of our inmost selves, we realize we're touchingly alike. We share similar yearnings and through love glimpse that image of God in which we are created. With newfound clarity, we realize our perceived separateness may be more perception than actuality. Our intimacy lets us glimpse a truer reality of how deeply we are alike, even in our deepest longings. We both hear the coyote's call. We both cry out into the night for that which we think we've lost. And we both see a glimmer of sacred love and presence in the other.

Spiritual Practice
LABYRINTH

A labyrinth is a nonbranching path without tricks or dead ends that is found in many cultures and religious traditions. There are diverse patterns, from the earliest Greek labyrinths of 2500 BCE, to the medieval labyrinths laid in the floors of cathedrals in France and Italy, to contemporary designs.

There are many ways to experience the labyrinth as you walk or trace a printed labyrinth path with your finger from the outside entrance to the center and back out again. The intricate Chartres Cathedral labyrinth begins at the periphery and winds through multiple 180-degree turns that bring you tantalizingly close to the center only to send you back out to the periphery. It is a metaphor and a tangible experience of a spiritual journey—of following an unknown path, of seeming U-turns, of coming close to the center only to find you are back on the edge. The journey inward to the center is often described as a time to release, offer up, and let go, while the center is a still place to listen and receive. The return path can be a time of integration as steps are retraced that connect the quiet center with the outside world.

In the context of this book, the labyrinth can be a prayerful way to further explore gift and loss in your life.

- Pause at the entrance before walking or tracing a labyrinth pattern with your finger. Release your concerns to God. Let go of any preset expectations. Take some slow, deep breaths. Quiet your mind.
- When ready, pray for awareness and an open heart, then enter the labyrinth. Find a pace that is natural and comfortable.
- Take with you a difficult loss in your life. As you experience the multiple turnings of the complex path, hold both the gift and your pain at its loss as loosely as you can. Hold them both out to God.
- When you reach the center, remain there for as long as you wish. This is a quiet place of rest, meditative openness, and prayerful listening.

∽ Pause before you leave, take a deep breath, and give thanks. Then retrace your steps back out into the world.

Exploring Deeper

Nature's changing seasons teach us about ourselves and about how to hold things.

∽ Give yourself the gift of time for reflection. Perhaps you can go out, or sit by a window where you can see outside. Take a few deep breaths. Consciously let go of worries and concerns. Arrive in this present moment, in this present season.

∽ Carefully observe everything outside. How would you describe this season? What do you love about this time of year? What do you not like?

∽ What will change with the coming of the next season? What will be lost? How easily can you let go of what you love about this time of year? Are there things that you hold tightly?

Sometimes we need to step back from our relationships to be aware of the astounding changes over time. This is an invitation to think about our long-term family relationships and friendships.

Family

∽ Picture the people in your family. What were they like when you first knew them? How have they changed? How have you changed?

∽ What was your relationship like last year, a decade ago, several decades ago? What is it like now? What has changed in your relationship?

∽ What losses have occurred over the years in your relationship? Were they easy or difficult? What things have you found easy to let go of? What has been difficult to let go of?

Friends

- Picture the face of a close friend. When did you first meet? What drew you to each other? What continues to hold your friendship together? What qualities do you admire in your friend? Can you describe your friend's difficult traits? How would your friend describe you?

- What has changed in your friendship over the years? What losses have happened? Which ones were easy to let go of? Were some difficult to let go of?

Holding

- Imagine yourself holding a family member or friend in your hands. What is the position of your hands? Do they grasp tightly? Or are they loosely cupped?

- What about your relationship? How do you hold it?

Pray

*It's hard
to risk change.*

*I clutch outgrown ways,
blanched grip strangles illusive security.*

*Can I love
enough to
welcome sacred
wind's fresh blowing?*

*For new beginnings God,
teach me
open hands.
Amen*

Relationships That Unravel and Tear Apart

A voice is heard in Ramah,
lamentation and bitter weeping.
Rachel is weeping for her children;
she refuses to be comforted for her children,
because they are no more.

Jeremiah 31–15

I blink my eyes and all I love is gone.... No good-byes.
No considerations. My life will never be the same. I
inhale and I am a mother and wife: I exhale and
there is utter darkness and I am a grieving widow
with no child to hold ...

A tidal wave has swept over me and I am trying to
hold it back with my bare hand. I cry from so deep
inside of me ... deeper than I've ever known. I cry
because my hand is so small and the wave so powerful. I am not strong enough. I am at the bottom of a
black pit, and I don't care.

Paula D'Arcy, Gift of the Red Bird:
A Spiritual Encounter

Some of our most difficult losses occur when we unexpectedly lose pivotal relationships, from our former best friend with whom we no longer seem to have anything in common, to our boss who no longer supports our work. Other relationships come with a natural life span— like friendships with our fellow school volunteers after our children have graduated from high school or our bond with trusted mentors after we've mastered their teachings. Particularly wrenching is the loss of one of our treasured relationships, such as a spouse who wants a divorce or a loved one who dies.

In this chapter, we'll explore our losses when a close relationship unravels or is torn apart.

Friendships with a Life Span

Sometimes, shared life experiences bond us together—and particularly intense experiences can forge tight connections. These friendships are healthy and nourishing, and we delight in their gift. They are so life giving that we assume they will last forever. But when our shared experience ends, we are often left startled and bereft as the relationship passes, surprised that there's no longer enough commonality in our lives to sustain a close friendship.

SCHOOL

Kim is lonely and homesick far from home her first college semester. Her life quickly intertwines with the life of equally homesick Olya as they study together, and later, as they share a house, friends, disagreements, and moments of mutual support. An intense friendship blossoms during their college years as they grow into young adulthood together. As they finish their degrees, each woman is eager again for adventure, and graduation brings a big-city job for Olya and two years of volunteer work in Africa for Kim.

As they go off on their new journeys, each young woman finds herself once again alone in an unfamiliar place. Olya sends pictures of the city, her apartment, and the crazy bargains she finds to furnish it. Kim sends pictures of her rural village and the shy smiles of the children she teaches. How can she describe the strangely different foods and simplicity of living, the relaxation of time and the gently elongated ways people greet each other? The rhythm of life has a beat as distinct as the lilting flow of this new language. It is unlike anything she has known before.

Both women become absorbed in their new lives. As their daily experiences diverge, there is less they can share. Kim cannot fathom Olya's big city; Olya cannot comprehend Kim's African village.

Kim and Olya's extraordinary day-to-day closeness and youthful immersion in each other's lives ended with graduation. Now living in vastly different worlds that cannot be shared, their distinctive experiences form them in increasingly dissimilar ways. There is a bewildering ache of loss as they mourn the surprising end of their intimate friendship.

But there are renewing gifts even in this loss. Once a friendship is gone, we often look back in astonishment and newfound appreciation. We can unwrap and more fully receive the present of this relationship. The hard-won knowledge that a singular time in life and its profound relationships are limited can let us savor the experience more fully. Understanding we will never again receive such gifts offers clarity of vision and allows us to recognize the transience of other gifts as they unfold. We learn the sacred art of relishing every moment precisely because these gifts will not last. This is a reckless, risky, passionate way to inhale deeply of the breath of life, and then to let it go just as freely.

There are other gifts of those college years. Though different experiences now draw them apart, their years of exceptional closeness and caring laid a priceless foundation. Kim and Olya's friendship was grounded at a more profound depth than day-to-day sharing. Their established trust will let them turn to each other at significant passages later in life. They may participate in each other's wedding, exchange baby pictures, or phone each other as they navigate life's turbulent waters. In their graying years, their shared vulnerability as their parents die and as they themselves age will have a poignancy that comes only from their early closeness.

Our early relationships and loves are less clouded by wounds from later experiences. We don't craft such impenetrable masks to hide our vulnerability. These friendships can retain that special sweetness of youthful openness throughout our lives. A relationship on which we teethed the meaning of mutual friendship—and through which we grew into adulthood—can keep the same innocent "I can tell you anything" quality thirty-five years later, even though we are only rarely in touch.

Passions and Projects

Sanjay and Matt attend the emotional meeting in response to a group in their town that has been mailing inaccurate, hate-filled flyers about minorities to every resident, writing vehement letters to the newspaper, and conducting high-profile parades that have given the community an unwelcome national reputation. That night, the community founds a task force to protect human rights.

Previously strangers, Sanjay and Matt now exchange daily e-mails and engage in frequent conversations as the crisis grows. A deep friendship springs from the depths of their shared concern and compassion. After several years of intense work, the community has rallied around the cause of human rights and educational programs are in place. The hateful mailings and letters have stopped as the group disbands. The community takes a deep breath of relief.

But paradoxically, there is also loss. From an intense relationship forged on daily conversation and shared beliefs, Matt and Sanjay now speak infrequently and run into each other only occasionally. Their lives no longer intersect at a common purpose and conviction.

Relationships that germinate in the rarefied air of shared compassion take us beyond ourselves and invite us to be our best selves. We glimpse our created-in-the-image-of-God selves and receive a profound inner vision of our true identity. Such relationships are sacred gifts that bear life-giving fruit.

But extraordinary friendships can end—even those that bestow rare company as we work together out of mutual compassion. Emotions ranging from a "let down" feeling to significant grief are experienced when we no longer have frequent, communal involvement. We learn a profound lesson to fully receive these uncommon gifts with gratitude, and to gracefully let them go.

Interrupted Relationships

As I wait for a red light, a bumper sticker reminds me, "The only constant in life is change."

Life is indeed about persistent change. Our lasting relationships must flex and adapt with our inner transformations. In addition, the continual alteration of the world around us powerfully impacts us and our relationships. In the midst of so much movement, some relationships we thought would endure for a lifetime come to an end. As life's constant of change asserts itself, even intimate relationships we anticipated would deepen over the years stretch beyond their breaking point. This happens within families, between close friends, and within communities. We are left hurt, angry, and alone with baffling and grievous losses of relationship.

Any of our nourishing, intimate relationships can flounder on rocks of change internal to the relationship. One person may not accept the inevitable changes in another and stubbornly cling to old ways of relating, constricting the relationship until it is no longer life giving and eventually withers and dies. Or one person can change so radically that the amount of energy and flexibility for a new way of relating is overwhelming. Sometimes one person withdraws from the relationship or it becomes abusive, hurtful, and unhealthy. And sadly, given enough time and enough relationships, we will experience betrayal. The shock of another's violation of confidence and trust is wounding in itself and often brings about the relationship's demise.

Besides navigating internal relational rocks, we can be caught in the perpetual whirlpool of changes in the external world. Outside storms pull, strain, and can break even our closest bonds.

People move to distant places. When we no longer see each other, previously strong friendships lose their vibrant immediacy, which frequent phone calls and e-mails cannot restore. Such geographic moves weaken even tight family ties as grandparents become strangers who infrequently visit their grandchildren. And despite heartfelt vows that we will keep in touch, long-distance moves mean the dissolution of our relationships within communities.

Sometimes people form new relationships. Our good friend meets a delightful other and as they spend time together, a fresh friendship or even a romance is born. Our friend no longer has the time or energy to sustain prior ties.

Folks become immersed in more demanding work schedules, new-found interests, travel, or the arrival of a grandchild. Our once-intimate friend no longer spends time with us. The one we relied on in the community is no longer free to help with projects. Our family member is not in town for the usual holiday dinners.

Difficult situations befalling one person can stretch a fulfilling relationship beyond the strongest glue that can hold it together. A friend may face life-altering physical change or depression, become consumed with caring for an ailing family member, withdraw into worry over financial concerns, or become distant as they grieve their own losses. In spite of our earnest desire to continue in a relationship, the other simply cannot participate and we grow apart.

When any serious relationship with a loved one prematurely ends, our losses are multilayered and anguished. The gift of each of our close relationships is unique, so mourning from their unanticipated dissolution is a one-of-a-kind journey. But with the unexpected demise of any committed relationship, we also share similar and very human patterns of loss and grief. These similarities bridge the unforeseen end of significant friendships, crucial family relationships, or deep relationships with a community.

We learn the pain-filled lesson that some cherished relationships are not ours forever. These losses teach us how to crawl and then walk through grief. We learn to name our losses and acknowledge their depth. We learn to mourn them fully before we can let them go. Our journey through this difficult terrain can bestow gifts that come disguised in very unpleasant wrappings. Our travel through grief acquaints us with a landscape we will surely see again with the death of anyone we love. Perhaps the terrain will not be so terrifying if we've experienced it before.

To shed light on our common patterns of loss when any close relationship ends, let us walk through the anguished unraveling of a marriage and the losses of divorce.

We often eat supper with Eric and Cho at their house or ours. One evening, after the children are tucked into bed, they tell us they are separating. I hadn't a clue. Concerned about the ripples such news would make in our small community, they had held their pain and struggle very closely.

When I later talk with Cho, she's surprisingly calm. She has wrestled with the idea of divorce for over a year and says all her tears have been cried. Her losses began a long time ago, as Eric's absence from family life has been a recurrent, stinging reminder that they are a second choice for him.

She has "tried on" the idea of not being Eric's wife anymore, of being a single parent, of having a marriage that didn't last. She's been angry, afraid, and hurt as she's worried about her future and that of her children. She's had time to name and accept the losses of divorce and has already begun the long process of grieving her marriage.

One person is often aware of serious trouble in a relationship before the other and may hold their anxiety close, unsure of its validity—it is frightening to acknowledge and confront such grave worries. But the withholding adds more strain to the relationship and leads to further isolation and loss of intimacy. Eventually, a conversation ensues: perhaps the couple can make positive change in their cherished relationship.

Cho's fear about their marriage finally prompts a talk with Eric, who is well respected and rapidly advancing in his career. Cho tells him she aches for the husband she used to have, recalling their early years of marriage as they delighted in each other's company and talked for hours about anything and everything. She reminds him of their surprise "dates" after the wedding and of Eric's unbounded joy and enchantment with their first baby.

But things have changed. With Eric's growing success, he works evenings while Cho and the children eat supper without him. At home, he receives numerous work-related phone calls. He assures his family, "This will just take a minute. You go on without me. I'll join you later." But he rarely shows up. Three months ago, he was so late for their son's birthday party that most of the guests had already left.

Eric hears her pleas. Then the phone rings. He grabs
his coat and says, "This will only take a few minutes ..."

When gnawing worries are shared but the other does not acknowledge their gravity or work toward resolution, something shifts. There is an agonizing loss of trust, mutuality, and support in any kind of relationship.

There is also somber affirmation of the severity of the problems. Eric and Cho come from vastly different childhoods. They view career, child-raising, and their relationship from distinctive perspectives.

> *Raised in a desperately poor family, Eric still feels shame*
> *from teasing about his hand-me-down clothes and vows*
> *his wife and children will never experience that aching*
> *poverty. His children will have warm winter coats and*
> *good shoes and music lessons; they will have the chance*
> *to play on sports teams.*
>
> *Eric also relishes being competent and rock-solid reli-*
> *able in his career. He wishes his father could have*
> *known his success before he died. He's frustrated when*
> *Cho asks him to come home early for their daughter's*
> *soccer game, or to take a long lunch hour for their son's*
> *school play. She doesn't seem to understand the tremen-*
> *dous stress he feels to be always available.*

My husband and I are not the only ones reeling from this announcement. Cho only told Eric a few months ago that she wants a divorce, and Eric is absorbing the enormity of this shock with disbelief. As they enter marriage counseling, Eric is overwhelmed by the prospect of losing his family, while Cho, who has already mourned the losses and stepped into a future without her husband, is comfortable with the possibility of divorce. Eric, meantime, continues to grapple with heart-wrenching loss and an uncertain future.

> *Eric feels blind-sided, betrayed by Cho's desire for divorce. His trust is at rock bottom. He deeply loves the children, and divorce cheats him of family even though he provides much of their financial support.*

There's a big difference between being the partner who initiates divorce and the one who's left behind. Both leaving and being left are saturated with loss, but from two markedly different perspectives.

> *As Eric and Cho enter into the tension of raising their children in separate households, mourning their marriage is complicated by their continuing presence in each other's lives. Though their marriage ends, a remnant of relationship continues as they jointly provide for their children. They see each other at school events, birthday parties, and handing off the kids. They hear of each other's activities through mutual friends and the children. And they must share personal details of their lives if it involves changing their times to be with the children.*

Eric and Cho's new relationship is convoluted, a delicate balancing act of high-wire precision. In *Ambiguous Loss: Learning to Live with Unresolved Grief,*[1] Dr. Pauline Boss, recognized for her groundbreaking research on ambiguous loss, describes this continuing relationship between divorced spouses as one of physical absence, but psychological presence. The fullness of grieving the end of their marriage is frozen by the ambiguity of their continuing relationship. Both partners exist in the limbo of a "not-yet" completely ended relationship.

The heartbreaking losses of interrupted relationships pull at a deep place within us. Intimate relationships are precious gifts we fervently desire to keep. These relationships do not have a discernible life span, and we could never predict their bewildering loss. But change happens. The passing of important relationships invites us across the threshold into grief.

We look, unblinking, through the layers of our losses to name and mourn them. We will recognize this terrain when someone we love dies, for we grieve the death of relationships and the death of people in similar ways.

The Irrevocable Loss of Death

There is no loss as wrenching, as irrevocable and complete, as the death of one whom we love. Just as the severing of our umbilical cord at birth is irreversible separation, so too is the finality of death. The depth of our wondrous God-given ability to love will be the terrible depth of our grief at its loss.

THE LOSS OF A CHILD

"He's dead. I'm sorry. I'm so very sorry."

I had said those searing words to strangers—how many times? Now they're said to me and my husband. How do we say good-bye to our third son, when we've not said hello? The pain takes my breath away, threatening to drown me. It shakes my foundations, leaving creation tilted at bizarre angles. Daffodils are no longer yellow, music is no longer something to get lost in, silence is no longer bearable. Life is monochromatic, flat. Many times I've sat with people in such pain, but I've never walked its suffocating depths.

Cold Hebrides wind blows across the Sound of Iona off the coast of Scotland. It is years after his death. I sit on my heels like women in developing countries as I watch the beach. Blue-green water of the sound's depths turns frothy gray as waves break upon the sand. Each wave inches up the beach and reaches a little closer to the names I've written in the sand. Under the Celtic crosses of my ancestors, I pray and give thanks for Colin's life. I sit for hours. Slowly the tide claims our names; Gary,

Nancy, Ian, Adam, Graham ... and Colin. All these
years I haven't let go of Colin. My hands tightly clutch
the promise of his life that I thought was mine to grasp.

Sun sets. Wind chills. The sand is smooth. I unclench
my hands. He was never mine. He wasn't even mine to
hold and rock while alive.

The death of a child is a grief-filled loss that needs time, gentleness, and courage to walk through. But this loss is never finished with us, nor do we ever "complete" our mourning. The take-your-breath-away, searing pain of grief loses intensity over time, but there will always be a melancholy ache.

An hour after his twenty-first birthday, poet Ann Weems's son Todd was killed. Over a decade later, when asked whether the biblical Rachel, who has lost her children, can ever be comforted, Ann replied, "No. No, Rachel will not be comforted. Not here, not now, not in the sense of being ultimately comforted."[2] When a loved one dies young, the natural order of life is appallingly upended. The young are supposed to outlive the old. Parents expect to raise their children. Our grief in the face of such outrageous, premature finality is nearly unspeakable. We are forever changed by this loss. We are irrevocably shaped and formed into different people.

An old priest, wise in the ways of life and loss, sat with me decades later. He gently said, "Take Colin with you everywhere. Keep him close by at all times. Colin gives you compassion for the agony of other people's suffering. It is his painful gift to you."

The Loss of Parents

With poignancy that stuns, memories and emotions flood us when our father or mother dies. Their death tugs at the core of our being, for our parents were the first people who loved us and who taught us how to love. Their love gave us the strength and courage to leave home and undergirds our independent life still. It was their love that was strong and sure enough to freely let us go.

Our parent's death also triggers a surprising, childlike fear as our peek-a-boo learning collapses. This time they really have gone away, never to return. We can't run back home for reassurance. We'll never hear their voice or feel their embrace again. We will never again share a meal together, laugh over pictures, or send them a birthday card.

With a parent's death, we come full circle in the journey of a lifetime. Since the moment we were born, we've traveled far from perceived infantile oneness into claiming our birthed separateness and becoming an individual. The cutting of our umbilical cord began the process decades ago; the last step is the finality of death's unequivocal physical parting. The awful truth crashes into the midst of our apparent self-sufficient adultness. We truly venture out on our own.

Eight months after my father died, my mother passed away. At the time of her death, my brother, Kevin, a wonderfully mature, gratefully married, middle-aged man, said in a dazed voice, "We're all alone now."

Astonished by the intensity and bottomless depths of our loss at the death of our parents, we're plunged into mourning. Gone is the parent who knew us intimately from our very beginning and loved us intensely. Forever lost is one of the most crucial people in our lives, whom we loved in a unique way. The depth of our emotional attachment is the measure of our grief.

We see our remaining parent reel with his or her loss, alone in a radically altered world where sheltering walls have come crashing down. We now see the gift and tenuousness of our own life and ongoing relationships from a new perspective.

There are further losses. The death of a parent means we're the oldest generation, the next to die. Gazing squarely into our own mortality is a dose of reality that punctures our illusion that we're guaranteed a tomorrow. It is sobering, just as our previous times of shedding illusions have been, as we've gazed into the mirror to face the truth about ourselves.

We've walked this way of loss before, in smaller ways. There have been so many losses in our lives, from ordinary and insignificant to seemingly earth-shaking. We lost our first sacred home in its deepest sense. We lost our childhood home, our innocence, innumerable things and places, close relationships. With each day's succession of losses, one following another, we learn about journeying through the valley of the shadow of death. We learn to hold things and others lightly in gently cupped hands. We learn to say thank you each day. We learn we must name and acknowledge our losses before we can understand what we haven't lost. Then we can mourn our true losses. In due time, we learn to let go of our losses and not to clutch life, but to open our hands to let life flow through our fingers.

With a parent's death, our losses span our entire life. The final loss of our parent recollects all previous losses in this relationship. Echoing in our current grief are emotions from our decades-long leaving home, from tensions entailed with our breaking away, from ancient arguments and misunderstandings that are still surprisingly potent and alive. The full impact of our parent's diminishment in their later years now finally breaks upon us. As their health or mind failed, we lost our image of them as strong and vigorous protectors as we are thrust into caring for them. All our earlier losses are gathered up in this final loss of death; we must mourn them all.

From our grieving, we may receive a surprising transformation of our parent-child relationship. Through the lengthy process of mourning, we remember and reexperience our parent, turning over images of the years of our relationship. Now that they're gone, we can finally gaze on them with adult eyes and tender understanding to see them anew as people who tried and failed, fell down and got up, and loved us the best they could. Perhaps now we can fully say thank you for the good times and be grateful for the gifts. And perhaps this can be a time of healing as we let go of old wounds and express remorse for wounds we inflicted.

Now we open ourselves to our parent in a totally new way, taking them into us so they inhabit our inner world and internalizing the one we have loved, struggled with, and physically lost. They come to live within us now, where we can never lose them again.

My mother's dementia during the last years of her life took her away from us long before she physically died. From occasional forgetfulness to frequently repeated questions, the disease progressed until she did not recognize her family.

In those last years, the mother I once knew receded. Just as she could not recognize me, I could no longer recognize my mother in her. Though she sometimes looked at me with a puzzled glimmer of recognition, she was a stranger, and I couldn't find the woman who loved me with a love I couldn't fathom until I had my own child, the woman who taught me how to be a mother myself. I searched for the woman who believed in me even when I wasn't sure about myself, but always returned bereft. The forgetfulness of dementia seemed to cast its spell on all members of the family, and our memories of her in earlier times started to fade into monochrome sepia prints.

In due time after her death, though, I was surprised by the vibrancy of resurgent memories. The mother I remembered from childhood and the joyful grandmother of my own children returned in full living color, once again present, accessible, and accompanying me through my days. I sometimes pause to think how much she would enjoy a good meal we're having, or see her smile and ruefully shake her head at the backwoods way I dress, or laugh with her in sheer delight over my new baby grandson. Sometimes I have a conversation with her. Our lifelong tension over my outdoors wardrobe has deflated, and I occasionally wear one of her pins, a silver Celtic knot from Scotland. It is a rich and comforting symbol of her continuing warmth and close presence within my world.

Just like my mother's Celtic knot, an intricate pattern formed by one continuous thread, we travel through life's intricately woven pattern with our parents' death and now come full circle. We're astonished to find it all really is one uninterrupted thread—this journey from infant oneness, through claiming our separateness, to letting go of our old way of being physically present to one another, and finally receiving grief's surprising gift of internal closeness with our lost parent. Renewing gifts do indeed come from loss.

Perhaps the old lesson of peek-a-boo has an even more profound lesson to teach in our later years. They really haven't gone away, after all.

The Loss of a Spouse

Somehow, sometime, somewhere, everything that seemed so white-hot significant between us just slips away. Like an unconscious sigh, we let it go without even noticing. We have each lost so much in our long years of marriage. From such loss, the gift of a silent love emerges that doesn't need words. This gentle love accepts the other and quietly receives with open hands the gift of "what is" in this particular moment. It is enough to just be with each other. After all these years, it is the only thing that seems important.

> *Inexorably, given the gentle movement of days, I am called to visit Seamus as he is gravely ill from his lung disease. He and Kate will not celebrate another wedding anniversary together or share another birthday. Kate is grateful to be able to take care of Seamus in these last days. It is good to be together for whatever time is left.*

The death of our life partner is the last loss of our long relationship. Only now do we fully know the anguished depth of that which we promised so many years ago—to love each other "in sickness and in health, as long as we both shall live." Our wrenching loss will continue unfolding as we return to an empty house, eat supper alone, and sleep in a cold bed. We will mourn this loss every day until it is our time to die. The measure of our love will be the measure of our loss and pain. Now we know fully the costly price of love.

Valley Journeys

> *Even though I walk through the darkest valley,*
> *I fear no evil;*
> *for you are with me ...*
>
> PSALM 23:4

With each passing of one we love, a journey through the valley of the shadow of death looms ahead. We've walked here before in our everyday losses and dyings. We're familiar with the lonely emotions of all who traverse the valley floor—shock, bewilderment and disbelief, lament and hopelessness, anger and fear. This journey through grief will take us ... as long as it takes us. There are no shortcuts through the valley, no timetables for the passage. At times, this "valley" seems more like a narrow canyon with formidable walls above which ravens circle in silence. We must navigate through dark shadows as we walk every twist and turn of the chilling canyon floor. Sometimes the path seems to double back as we tread through the same emotions again and again in varying degrees of intensity.

Mourning the death of his wife, Joy, in *A Grief Observed,* British novelist C. S. Lewis states:

> Grief is like a long valley, a winding valley where any bend may reveal a totally new landscape ... (but) not every bend does. Sometimes the surprise is the opposite one, you are presented with exactly the same sort of country you thought you had left behind miles ago. That is when you wonder whether the valley isn't a circular trench. But it isn't.[3]

From deep within the valley of death's shadow, we may hear a coyote howling once again in the dark of night. And on more than one occasion, we might find ourselves wistfully calling out our longing for what we've lost into the wind. Woven into our grieving is the deeper mourning and primal yearning for our sacred home—some of my African friends speak of death as a homecoming. As we feel our way alone through the valley of mourning, our longing for God and divine presence is acute. It seems we are very far from home.

The only way to embrace the rest of our lives is to journey completely through this valley of grief. The choice is ours. We can cling to our loved one and bury our future with him or her. Or we can unclench our hands and let this person go. Mourning is the lengthy process of accepting the finality of physical loss of our loved one, so that we can continue our journey in the land of the living. Eventually, we will come out on the far side of our grief. Towering canyon walls shorten into rounded hills that flatten further still. And the valley floor widens out into a light-filled land of acceptance.

We are forever changed by our valley sojourn. Our hands finally let go of the one we've physically lost and are open to receive the continuing gifts of future life.

> *As I leave the trauma room to somehow tell a young wife that her husband has died, I'm pulled into a room to deliver a baby whose wet black hair is already crowning into this world. I suspect death and life, constantly juxtaposed, are separated by much less than a wall between emergency department rooms. In the great inhalation and exhalation of the cosmos, they are really one word: death-birth. Experiencing death-birth opens a fissure in our everyday world through which we glimpse eternity.*

Here again is the difficult learning that something in us must die for new birth to happen. After naming and fully acknowledging what we've lost, after crying our tears of mourning for as long as it takes, we must let go of the gift we've lost to accept the gift of the next moment. The alternative is to entomb our losses and roll the burial stone firmly against the entrance, memorializing the loss of one we loved in a stone-cold tomb and closing ourselves off in their dark burial place to hang onto fading memories. This is a way of death. This is a path of burying our present life alongside our loved one in the grave.

There is a different path we can walk. After we gaze unflinchingly into the terrible depths of our loss, we name everything that's been torn from our hands and journey the valley of death's shadow to become a radically changed person. We can let the stone be rolled away from the tomb of our loss to expose our anguish to the wind of God, hovering over the deep, waiting to breathe new life into being and to create once again. This way does not bury our pain and our loss, but beckons us to accept it. The one we loved is rewoven afresh into our daily life, awakening as a life-giving presence within our self to accompany us every step of our journey.

Sun's light floods a now-empty tomb. We stand with hands open to God's possibilities of life anew.

Spiritual Practice
ACCOMPANIMENT

The loss of people we love and cherish precipitates our anguished travel through grief. This passage will take more time than we want to give and will lead us into shadow lands where we do not wish to go. It is a lonely journey as we each walk our unique path. Others cannot walk the depths with us, but they can take our hand and sit with us for a moment. We will need such people along the way.

Others have walked this way before and left footprints in the valley floor. Their wisdom, either spoken to us or left behind in books, can provide food for this difficult travel. Scripture, religious leaders, and people wise in the ways of our tradition can open our eyes to cairns along the way.

A spiritual director can help us listen for the Spirit's whisper or nudge or provision, or simply sit with us in God's unfathomable silence. He or she can accompany us as we name and grieve our losses, and when the time is appropriate, to open our hands and let them go.

Spiritual direction is accompaniment by another who listens with us for God's presence in our lives. It's not so much about being "directed," but rather about being supported as we intentionally pay attention to the sacred. Spiritual direction training programs or the regional offices of the tradition in which you worship may keep lists of spiritual guides in your area. A listing by geographic region of spiritual companions who are members of Spiritual Directors International is on their website, www.sdiworld.org. This website also has helpful descriptions of spiritual direction and questions that you can ask a prospective spiritual companion or guide.

People come alongside us for a moment, but then we continue our travel through the valley on our own. But many discover they are not alone. People meet God in this valley—not the God they used to know, the dressed-up, pretty God of stained-glass windows or renaissance art, the God who smiled on a life untouched yet by deep grief—but rather a presence that walks dark, cold canyons of loss, a presence that is beyond image or words.

Exploring Deeper

Interrupted Relationships and Death

It is painful to lose a serious relationship that we envisioned would continue for our lifetime. Some parts of our loss are obvious, but others are hidden and pull at our most vulnerable selves. It often takes an entire lifetime to explore, name, and grieve these considerable losses. As passing years bestow gifts of distance, maturity, and wisdom, we are often invited to spiral again and again through grieving these losses.

A door may open in later years, a portal only available as we grow older. When we are able, we can revisit these tender, wounded places of loss. But this time we bring our older selves. This time we bring the self who has experienced more of life's daily losses, the self who has let go of so much, the self who has received sacred, renewing gifts and the costly gift of loving compassion for bruised places deep within ourselves and others. Each journey through these pain-filled places lets us go a little deeper, but only as deep as we are able at any given time. It is vitally important to honor and respect where we can walk—and where we cannot yet walk.

Interrupted Relationships

- ❧ Find a quiet, safe, and comfortable space. It may be indoors and enclosed by well-loved surroundings. Or it may be a secluded outdoor place or a little-used walking trail. It is important to be in a space where you will not be interrupted.

- ❧ Remember a cherished relationship you've lost. Picture the other. How would you describe that person to someone who had never met him or her? What did you love about this person? What were his or her difficult traits?

- ❧ It can take much courage to bring back memories of the other. This may be enough for now. In truth, this step may take years to fully enter into.

> ✎ If it is appropriate to continue, name what you lost when this relationship ended. Have you mourned this loss? How do your hands hold this loss? Are they grasping it tightly, holding it loosely, or have they let it go?
>
> ✎ What was not lost with the end of this relationship? Are you aware of any gifts that you might have received after this relationship ended?

Death

Enter into this exploration if it is helpful and the time is ripe. Walking through tender losses can bring gifts of insight and healing, but only when we're ready.

> ✎ Remember the one whom you loved dearly and lost. Can you visualize this person? What did he or she look like?
>
> ✎ Can you name all things you loved about this person?
>
> ✎ What were some of your loved one's challenging characteristics? Did you struggle with certain of his or her habits, viewpoints, or behaviors?
>
> ✎ Rest with these remembrances. Letting the other gently back into your life and into this space may be enough for now. Perhaps it will be enough for many months or even years ahead.
>
> ✎ What did you lose when your loved one died? Have you grieved this person's passing? Can you describe the longing of your heart for him or her?
>
> ✎ If you visualize your hands holding your loved one, are your hands closed or open?
>
> ✎ If you wish to continue: Is your loved one a part of your life—not in the physical way you used to experience but in the sense of a felt presence? Can you describe that presence? When are you most aware of your loved one? Do you interact with him or her? How does your loved one's presence influence you?

Pray
LAMENT PSALM

How long O God
must I walk this valley of tears?

By day, I wander in shadows
on the canyon's floor.
By night, I shiver in
the cold.
A coyote howls.
I cry out in the dark

I've wandered so far.
My heart aches
for home
where I know you wait for me.
Amen

When Foundations Shake and Crumble

> Every question possessed a power that was lost in the answer.... Man comes closer to God through the questions he asks ...
>
> *Moishe the Beadle in Elie Wiesel's* Night

> Now there was a great wind, so strong that it was splitting mountains and breaking rocks in pieces before the Lord, but the Lord was not in the wind; and after the wind an earthquake, but the Lord was not in the earthquake; and after the earthquake a fire, but the Lord was not in the fire; and after the fire a sound of sheer silence.
>
> *1 Kings 19:11–12*

The story of the losses of our lives begins with our first breath and continues in persistent rhythm until we breathe our last breath. This long view offers insight and guidance as we face particularly painful losses of well-being, security, and beliefs. A larger perspective helps illuminate our path on these difficult parts of a journey we did not choose.

Roller Coaster Ride: Physical Well-Being

> *"It's a roller coaster. I didn't buy a ticket, never wanted a ride. First they say everything is okay, surgery removed the tumor. Later they say everything isn't totally okay, that I need chemotherapy—just a precaution. But in those months of chemo, I receive a gift of sorts. I learn I'm not indispensable at work. It's freeing, actually, as so much of my identity came from work. But now who am I? I yearn to meet the self who is defined neither by work nor by a brush with cancer."*

Mariam talks openly about her fearful encounter with a potentially fatal illness. Her taken-for-granted health is shattered and her professional image is turned inside out. When she looks in the mirror, the face staring back is not the person her mind's eye expects to see. Who is she now? Her cancer demands that she look deep for an unexplored identity hidden beneath her previous mental image.

> *"The roller coaster careens downward. Years later, lung nodules show up on my scan.*
>
> *I'm scared. Angry. This isn't fair—everything was supposed to be okay. Oh, I can keep taking chemotherapy, hopeful for remissions. But the cancer will keep recurring. I will die of it.*
>
> *Who am I? I still refuse to be defined by my disease or by my losses. I'm no longer the person who used to be in control, who had energy to take care of tasks and other people. Rather I'm the one who needs care. I'm the one who is vulnerable. This is not an identity I choose. Buried inside are losses that need to be cried out. This is a long mourning process."*

Loss of physical well-being steals our identity built on being physically strong, on feeling good, and being full of energy. We watch this previ-

ous self slip through our fingers inside the EMI scanner and drain out
as chemotherapy drips through an IV tube into our veins.

But even worse, fatal illness steals our future. We must venture into
this unknown terrain bereft of the tomorrows that we assumed would
be ours.

> *"I finally let go of my control and let myself be vulner-
> able and cared for by others. When I learn to receive
> their care with profound gratitude, I receive the greatest
> gift. I realize how much I am loved. It's extraordinary.
> This love lets me be even more vulnerable. It finally lets
> me release little concerns and being so busy with work.
> I don't have to row so hard every day.*
>
> *"My advice? Relish the goodness in every day. Delight
> in the smell of green grass and the warmth of sun, laugh
> with your friends, let go of everything else. I'm in soli-
> darity now with others through this experience of love—
> with those who hurt and with creation as I'm aware of
> being part of God's natural rhythm of ebb and flow."*

It is agonizingly difficult to let go—to name and mourn our loss of control and health at a much-too-early age. We peer into a dark abyss
where we cannot see the bottom or the way ahead. But once we let go,
a different way of seeing is given. With less time left, the time that
remains is priceless. The sense of each day's treasure is heightened and
perfected to let us relish the glorious taste, sight, sound, and feel of each
moment's gifts. Something in us breaks open as we begin to savor this
ordinary, extraordinary life that bestows such extravagant presents as
green grass, sunlight, and laughter.

After a life-changing accident, middle-aged Benjamin talked with me:

> *"One moment I'm driving. The next thing I know, I
> wake up in the ICU, days later. I know it's bad, really*

bad. I've never been taken care of before. But there's no choice—I have to just accept it, to accept what is. Others clean me, feed me, change my gown, and make decisions for me. Later, at home, people help me dress, drive me to appointments, and fix my food.

"But in my devastating loss, I am also given a gift. When I allow others to support, love, and care for me, when I gratefully embrace their presence, there is an unexpected sweetness. I feel their fierce love. God's love is vibrant in their love. And God's presence is in the moment-to-moment goodness, beauty, and magnificence of this world. An intense awareness of the blessing of life fills me. When I'm so depleted and weak, I'm also most intensely aware of the blessings given to me. I receive gifts—I can breathe, see, hear, and speak. In attending to the gifts of the moment, I'm overwhelmed with gratitude, particularly for small things—very small things—such as a sandwich for lunch.

"This is the key to recovery, to 'heart' recovery. My being 'fine' is not tied to the external physical markers of being okay. The accident gives me clarity that the gift of life is so great, there's no time to be petty, small, or negative. Rather, we're to live into the largest of God's astounding gift of life."

To lose physical health, abilities, and self-image is a grievous loss that we must name and mourn. Such overwhelming loss challenges us to search for a more profound identity, which is not defined by our physical well-being—or by its loss. It is a paradox that when we are vulnerable, we can more fully receive life's greatest gift—the astonishing gift of love. Our masks, protective barriers, illusions of "having it together," and our false sense of self-sufficiency keep love from penetrating our deepest being. But tangible expressions of human love, like help with dressing, a sandwich, a get-well card, or a ride to the doctor's office—gifts bestowed on us when we're most helpless—can awaken us to the love that binds us all together at our most exposed level, beneath all our surface bravado.

Human love lets us glimpse divine love, that birthright love for which we yearn. Being vulnerable breaks us open to our most profound being, the self created by and loved by God. We are fiercely loved because we were created in sacred love. Period. In tearful acceptance, we can let the love of God and others gently rain on us and soak into our driest, most thirsty depths. We who are created in the image of God can love one another and be loved with sacred intensity. We experience a larger identity, one of solidarity, as Mariam so beautifully puts it, "with others through this experience of love; with those who hurt and with creation" as we are part of nature's endless ebb and flow.

Losing the Illusion of Security

Parents and teachers train us to protect ourselves, to be prudent, and to build safeguards into our lives. But many religious traditions—and life itself—teach us just the opposite: We need to be open and vulnerable, to trust in something other than ourselves. No matter how much planning we do, we are not in control.

A window is forced open and our house is burglarized. Our friend is mugged in the city, a little girl disappears while walking to school, another inner-city shooting is on the newspaper's front page. Around the globe, gunshots ring out, land mines explode, and bombs are dropped in acts of piracy, terrorism, and war.

Hackers steal our identity, a virus crashes our hard drive, unwanted phone calls and text messages invade our privacy. National and global economies ebb and flow and crash as we watch our life savings hemorrhage. At work, we are downsized and told to clean out our office.

Volcanoes spew ash skyward and bubble up molten lava. Green skies warn of tornados that rip through towns, while hurricanes, tsunamis, and floods drench everyday lives. Fires roar through buildings and forests, earthquakes shake homes into rubble, and drought silently steals life as babies and children cry from hunger.

Life is obscenely exposed as a ridge walk where terrain plummets dizzily downward on either side. All our moats, barrier walls, and safeguards can be breached. We are not invulnerable. Eruptions of both creation and humankind can harm, even kill us, and those we dearly love.

Our illusion of control is shattered. Reality's undertow pulls us under the surface of the delusion of human-made security. If we can neither control life's explosions nor guarantee safety from them, how do we live day to day? If our fantasy of a protected life rests on quicksand, upon what beliefs and understandings can we ground our lives?

We wrestle with pivotal questions. Easy answers and simple plati-tudes do not work in the maelstroms of real life. As we confront the loss of our notions of control and physical security, our deepest beliefs are challenged.

Losing Beliefs and Identity

Early in life, firm beliefs ground us. Certain principles and values form us and guide us through myriad decisions and actions. Clear ideals pro-vide meaning and purpose and give us identity. Rock-solid faith in the tradition in which we worship tethers us tightly. Our fervent beliefs anchor us in a world of shifting sand and flowing water.

But a day may unexpectedly dawn when the moorings of our convic-tions slip. We go from confident walking propelled by our beliefs to blind groping in the dark or even to paralyzed immobility. It can hap-pen gradually over time. Life experiences repeatedly crash against our certainty and undermine our beliefs until they collapse.

Or it can happen all of a sudden, like a hand on the light switch. One moment we live guided by the brilliant incandescence of moral values, ideals, or faith. Then—click. What we believed and hoped is extinguished, replaced by an impenetrable blackness that appears even darker to our unaccustomed eyes.

Ideals may shatter when we devote part of our lives to an endeavor that crumbles and fails. Our sense of purpose and meaning may be destroyed when we wholeheartedly believe in a community, tradition, or country revealed to be far less noble than we had thought. Surface-deep faith is ripped open when our loved one skids off into eternity on a lonely stretch of slick road, when we hear a dreaded diagnosis in our doctor's office, or when the phone rings at home and a hospital chaplain asks us to come to the emergency department immediately.

Beliefs and ideals are intangible, yet they form the spine of our lives. They grant us significance and identity, sustenance and vision beyond our own narrow horizons. When convictions are dashed against rock-hard life and disintegrate into pieces, we are left bereft of knowing who we are and why we get up each day.

Yet journeys guided by beliefs also traverse through fall and winter seasons. We walk the ever-present terrain of loss and death in our ideals, values, and faith. And we can emerge changed people in a landscape of new gift and mature growth.

THEN AND NOW

We all know people like Billy—he is every teenage boy or girl who is so on fire with idealism that they live on the periphery and advocate shaking the world apart to start over. They dress and act and talk in ways that are counter to social norms. They are passionate about creating a world based on fairness and compassion, where no one starves or dies from treatable disease, where we can finally learn to live together without the horror of war. Don't we all yearn for such a world?

After Billy graduates from high school, he slams into people who do not share his ideals and fight him aggressively. Billy confronts embedded social structures carefully built to support and maintain systems that oppose his deepest beliefs. He clashes with those who reap benefit from the status quo and powerfully obstruct any change.

Confrontation with reality is somber disillusionment. Ideals can become casualties as our life's foundation cracks and our hopes crumble around us. We are stilled and motionless, confused and despairing in an inner world of slack water where no tide flows in or out. Divested of illusions that previously guided our lives, we are left to journey bewildering, difficult terrain. This is a long, perilous passage. We will never be the same.

But then we run into William. Who would recognize Billy in this middle-aged man? He is beginning to bald, has a family and a modest house and owns his own business, which packages and sells dried beans, lentils, and rice to make basic, healthy soups and stews. The spark of the old Billy flashes as he tells us about his company that employs and teaches people who have been homeless and lack skills to find regular jobs. William retains a small long-term staff, but he measures success in the employees who stay a year or so and are then able to find other jobs.

William admits to hitting bottom after high school as he crashed into successive brick walls of opposition to his most-cherished ideals. He let go of his fiery conviction that he could shake the world and people into changing. This hard loss led him down paths of rage, sourness, and hopelessness and turned him into an angry, bitter man.

But eventually, he named and mourned the loss of his romanticized notions, and let them go. He stopped trying to control the world and other people. It was a journey that took many years, but in the end it transformed Billy into William. With his newly open hands, he received the gift of compassion. He is still passionate about his ideals and firmly grounded in trying to live them. But now he's motivated by love. He's creatively remodeled a small corner of the world and given life and hope to many who previously were without it.

Losing Faith

There have been questions all along—from innocent child questions as my father read me bedtime Bible stories, to raging adolescent and young adult questions that led me away from church, to theologically formed questions in seminary. People with devastating losses in my practice of medicine were disturbing questioners of a God of love, and my gnawing doubts cast themselves against the hard edges of church doctrine and creedal statements.

But I've been grateful for questions and for their struggle. The words of Moishe the Beadle, spoken before the horror of the transportation of Jews from their little town of Sighet in Transylvania, ring of deep wisdom for me. We come "closer to God through the questions." Questions, if examined, provide a portal to reflect upon our faith. But more important, they open a door into an encounter with the living God whose name we cannot pronounce as we stand before mystery.

By high school, I begin to wriggle out of the outgrown skin of my carefully taught childhood faith. I know Bible stories, songs, and how to worship Sunday morning. I am grateful as these have served me well while growing up. But childhood faith is not meant to address life's rocky places, and I must eventually climb out of the easy float down the river of simplified stories and catchy tunes. Both I and my faith must mature.

But there are wonderful childhood hours in the willow tree. I often climb high into the tree to spend the day in its branches. Sometimes this leafy world is hold-your-breath still; sometimes the wind rocks the branches. If I am completely quiet, I might receive something sweet—a sense of presence that would beckon me back.

I learned to pray properly in church and before supper, hands folded, with the right words. If that is prayer, what is it, exactly, that happens in the willow tree? I begin to think of it as "not being," as existing within this other presence. Swinging up to the sky, splashing in sunlit creek water, running fast as wind in moonlight—"not being" happens other times, a gift as sweetly given as summer and as innocently received. I don't know the name of the hand that rocks the tree, sparkles the water, or lights the moon. God lives at church. So this is ... not God?

I leave church, God's house of folded hands and worded prayer, in my teens, not to return for twenty-five years. But the gift of moments of "not being," of unnamed presence as close as breathing, does not leave me. These moments come while I study science at university and peer in a microscope, awestruck by the complexity and interweaving of creation. They come when I lie on my back in a field and watch stars stretched horizon to horizon, silenced by the mystery of the cosmos. They come in the first years of medical school, as the intricacy of life unfolds in astonishing beauty.

But in later years of medical school and residency, I see life smash into death in more ways than I ever wanted to know. Death extinguishes life split-second-sudden after a fateful decision while driving, when nighttime fire roars through a house, or in the crack of a gun being fired. Death also extinguishes life slowly, creeping by degrees as people die piece by piece. Ripped apart, the raw pain of people's suffering gapes open. I am invited to enter in.

It's overwhelming. There is no time, energy, or desire to tree-climb, creek-splash, or stargaze. I rock a child with end-stage cystic fibrosis as his brother dies of the same disease in the next bed. I daily change the oozing bandages of a young woman filleted open from chest to pubis by surgeons trying to stop a lethal infection. I treat a man whose life and spinal cord are blown apart by gunshots just outside the emergency department door. Each day brings more pain. The first baby I deliver is to a terrified twelve-year-old girl whose screams I will always hear. The baby has Down's syndrome.

We live in the inner city next to the hospital, a place where on Saturday morning the sidewalks are stained red from last night's knife fights. Our neighbors live in poverty. The children, eyes devoid of the sparkle of hope, come to my backdoor where we share the luxury of oranges together. I wonder, "Where does God live?"

Taking a graduate comparative religion class, I search for answers. For the first time, I read the Bible carefully, voraciously hungry for wisdom. I taste lines of Buddhist scripture, savor Zen meditation, and stretch into yoga asanas.

As mosque call sounds in a foreign land, the medical student says, "It's in Allah's hands." I stay with the patient in emergency as he leaves to pray. Later, the chair of medicine in this Muslim country hands me a small volume of Sufi poetry; intricate Arabic script, mesmerizing designs, and translucent pages of English translation are folded into it.

Reading the Sufis feels to me like coming home to a place I've never been. They dare put words to "not being." They risk speaking of overwhelming presence. I spend time in silence and ponder the Sufi's Allah, Sarah and Abraham, Ishmael and Isaac.

Questions from inner-city medical school about God's presence continue to haunt me. After a particularly severe winter while practicing medicine in Germany, I stop in the doorway of the Dachau building that houses the ovens. As I pause on the threshold, cold, dank air from inside the dark room flows outward and chills me to the bone. Where was God when the ovens were hot? Are there God-forsaken spaces in time, ground zero from which the fireball of god-lessness billows out to engulf people? I remember another heat, the shimmering heat of a drought-stricken country where gaunt mothers with milkless breasts hanging flat cradle stick-legged, swollen-bellied children with fly-bothered faces. Where does God live?

A woman silently hands me a book. No sparse kōan (paradoxical riddle) sayings, no Arabic script, no intri-cate illustrations. The chaplain at the hospital in England where I chair emergency services smiles. The Cloud of Unknowing, a book from earlier Christian tradition, is like falling down the rabbit hole into home. Once again I glimpse willow tree, "not being," sun-splashed creek water, wind in the moonlight, and unnamed presence. I wait in silence. Is this God of mys-tery also the God of the Celtic cross in my childhood Presbyterian church? Is this God of silence also the God of Bible stories that my church-deacon father read me every night? Is this God of yearning also the God of the church's worded prayer and folded hands?

It's been a long walk outside traditional stained-glass windows and candlelight. There are no easy answers. But I return to my roots, to the church of my ancestors with the Celtic cross.

Throughout my faith journey—and probably yours, too—there have been many questions and many losses. There have been multiple times to let go to receive new gifts. Life continually challenges past answers that we either formulate or are taught, that we cling to until one of life's tsunamis breaks them into pieces and sweeps them away. Pain and suffering confront faith and contest easy answers. We let go of well-worked formulas and clichés that fall apart in the face of real life, that address neither the complexity of life nor the depth of suffering. Letting go, we learn to humbly wait for the God who is, the God without a name who is only known as "I am," who refuses to be contained inside human-made boxes. The continuing loss of easy faith, faith filled with certainty and woefully inadequate conceptions of God, is the price of encounter with the God of mystery.

LOSING GOD IN THE DARK

Thomas sits across from me in this sacred, spiritual direction space in time.

"This is different. There is no life crisis that wipes out my platitudes of faith. This is more like a slow-motion sunset, where the sky's light slowly turns dark blue, then purple, then indigo, then pink. I look up and I'm startled by the darkening sky of my faith world. When did this happen? When did it become night? How long have I not been able to see?

"I've navigated my share of life crises. As a priest, I've accompanied countless others through their difficult places. But now, inexplicably, without any discernible cause, my faith is like the sun that has reached the western end of its arc in the sky ... and set.

"I am alone, in the dark. The God I used to 'know' has disappeared. The ways I used to name God no longer work. Prayer is dust-dry, lifeless. I wonder why I even try. Scripture words, once so vital and nourishing, no longer speak. I'm bereft, living under a pall of disturbing silence with no image, no sense of God. Church is a struggle. Whatever does it all mean? The way I used to believe

*is no longer valid—doctrine doesn't mean anything.
There are no answers."*

This slow slide into darkness is deeply disorienting. Sitting alone in the silence of this spiritual night, our hands cannot grasp or clutch anything. Our mind cannot create human-made constructs in which to house God. The comfort of our "knowing" all about God or soaking up the sweet consolations of prayer does not exist here. With hands pried open of self-assuredness, we approach the mystery of God. Thankfully, we cannot see in our usual way in the dark.

Years later, Thomas looks back and writes:

> *"There's a secret that you won't hear from most spiritual writers, in sermons, or at retreats. There will come a time when the God you thought you knew, who is proclaimed without end to be faithful, loving, and present, will leave. Really leave, not just take a brief vacation or play a quick game of hide-and-seek, but get on a bus and leave for good in a cloud of diesel exhaust. This is the stuff they don't tell you about in Sunday school.*
>
> *"As a teenager, I thought I'd 'found' God. God was perfectly clear, present, and unambiguous. I wholeheartedly believed. It didn't occur to me that God is not an object to be found like a personal teddy bear who only exists to be present, warm, and cuddly on our terms.*
>
> *"Later, much later, those unequivocal tenets of faith slip away as the god of sure answers and certainty disappears. Something deep within me becomes unmoored. I can no longer swim, assured of a destination and my power to get there. I float without bearings and rely on currents that take me where they will.*
>
> *"This is a heart-wrenching letting go of knowing God in a way I can name, describe, and control. These last*

years have been a slow, creeping blindness that inex-
orably leads into darkness. In the darkness there are no
answers to who God is, only the reality that God is."

Thomas grows accustomed to this place of not knowing, of not having
answers. With the loss of a god he can contain, perhaps even control,
comes a dramatic shift in his relationship with God. He learns to live in
the dark, leaving behind his expectations as he humbly shows up for
prayer. As he is defined by his relationship with God, when his understanding of God changes, his self-identity in relation to God must also
change. Sometimes, he's overtaken by a fearful desire to grab something
concrete about God that he can keep in his back pocket to bring out
whenever he needs.

> *"In this place of openness to God as God is, sometimes I*
> *panic. I realize I'm floating in the middle of the ocean*
> *at night. The ocean is God, and I'm floating in it. But*
> *then comes the fear that I'm sinking and will drown. I*
> *begin to thrash about and want to grasp at answers*
> *again. But there aren't easy answers. There is just the*
> *ocean that is God, and when I finally let go, the possi-*
> *bility of floating in it."*

This is the ultimate letting go, losing all our favored ways to describe,
contain, control, and experience God, and in the end, letting go of God.
Even on our spiritual journeys, the inescapable rhythm of gift and loss
and growth sounds.

In tender imagery that harkens back to our earliest gifts and losses,
St. John of the Cross describes God as:

> A loving mother who warms her child with the heat of her
> bosom, nurses it with good milk and tender food, and carries
> and caresses it in her arms. But as the child grows older, the

> mother withholds her caresses and hides her tender love ...
> and sets the child down from her arms, letting it walk on its
> own feet so that it may put aside the habits of childhood and
> grow accustomed to greater and more important things.[1]

St. John described this God-weaning, this being set down by God that leads us to "more important things," as a dark night. It seems dark to us, because this opening to God is not our visible doing, but rather God's movement hidden in darkness from our consciousness and our endeavors. Mother Teresa wrote to her spiritual director:

> If ever I become a saint, I will surely be one of "darkness" ...
> this terrible sense of loss—this untold darkness—this loneli-
> ness, this continual longing for God—which gives me that
> pain deep down in my heart—Darkness is such that I really
> do not see—neither with my mind or with my reason ...[2]

St. John describes the losses of this dark night as leading to sweet gift. But the gift we receive is not a return of confident knowing or past experiencing of God. Rather, as our hands are gradually opened to let go of our certainty about God and of our effort to "attain" God, we're given the gift of receiving God and awakening to an encounter with mystery. This is not the god who fits inside human constructs, about which we can speak with assured knowing. This is the ineffable God who is.

Spiritual Practice
LECTIO DIVINA

A slow, contemplative praying of scripture, *lectio divina* (sacred reading) is an ancient gift from early Christians. Throughout the centuries, this deep listening to scripture has been kept alive in the Christian monastic tradition. St. Benedict encourages us to "listen carefully … with the ear of your heart."[3] Like Elijah, who could not hear God's voice in wind, earthquake, or fire, we are invited to listen in the "sound of sheer silence" for God's word to touch our hearts. We can listen for God's still, small voice only when we and our minds are quieted into silent listening.

- Choose a quiet place without distractions. Offer your concerns to God and let go of them. Take a slow, deep breath, focus on your breathing. Settle into the silence.
- Slowly, reverently, read a short passage of scripture. Listen for a word or phrase that seems to have special interest for you, that captures your attention. You can read the passage several times, listening for God's word or phrase for you this day.
- Gently repeat the word or phrase, turn it over and ponder it, allow it to interact with your life: with your past memories, your anxieties and joys, your desires and hopes. Let the word(s) sink deep inside to touch you on a profound, personal level.
- Offer what has come to you—difficult experiences, new understandings—to God in prayer. Ask God what God is saying to you in this word or phrase. Wait and listen, allow yourself to be gently touched and changed by God's words.
- Silently, wordlessly, rest in the presence of God, as a small child rests in the arms of a parent.

Exploring Deeper

Loss of Well-Being

The loss of physical well-being shatters our illusion of control and invincibility. This is a sobering, difficult place for us. The following exercise invites you to sit with this disillusionment and to explore your thoughts and emotions.

- Settle into a quiet, peaceful place. Give yourself the gift of time. Recall concerns and tasks that await you, hold them one by one, then put them aside.
- Be aware of the details and textures and colors around you. Notice the silence and the sounds.
- Do you grieve the loss of anything physical? Have you yearned for well-being or physical wholeness from childhood? Has illness or accident taken something from you?
- What emotions or thoughts surface?
- Have other people ever taken care of you? How did they help you? What did you think or feel at the time? What about now?
- How did this loss affect your self-image? Who were you before? Who are you now?

Loss of Faith

The loss of beliefs and faith, our times of dark-walking through God's seeming absence shakes the deepest foundations of our lives. These are also invitations to ponder and go deeper in our spiritual journey.

- What is your earliest memory of God? Can you describe this God?
- What life experiences challenged this view of God? What did you lose? What emerged?
- How has your image of God changed over your life?

- Have you had times in your life where God seemed absent? What was that time like?
- What gifts have emerged from these losses?
- How do you describe God at this time in your life?

Pray

God
how I miss those days of playing
hide-and-seek with you
as I would run up laughing and touch you
standing stock-still in the noonday sun casting
*   no shadow,*
my solid, reliable, stable God.

But you began to hide and
the day lengthened and shadows played tricks
you would jump out and let me tag you again
before I was swallowed with fear
that you were gone for good
my trickster, fickle God.

Day has ended swallowed in night
no place to run in a place beyond sight
hiding with no way to seek
the game is over
as you whisper
"why do you expect to see me
when the tomb is empty?"

                              Sister Teresa Jackson, OSB

The Passing of Time:
Our Final Loss
... and Gift

8

All people are grass, their constancy is like the
flower of the field.
The grass withers, the flower fades ...

Isaiah 40:6–7

"Our bodies start dying before we're born," my medical school professor declared, startling me. In the springtime of life, I hadn't thought about my own aging, or pondered the certain arrival of autumn or the inevitable coming of winter in my life.

But the ticking clock that marks our aging is set when our first cells divide. The number of future cell divisions is not infinite. Our body's functioning is not indefinite. Limits are hard-wired into our anatomy: we are aging, and we will die.

With each rotation of the earth on its axis, the clock ticks one day. With each orbit of earth around the sun, one year passes. These movements cannot be undone and time cannot be unwound. Breaking an egg or burning a piece of wood teaches us that some things are irreversible and that the physical passing of time is a one-way street.

But we love to fantasize that this might not be true. We envision time machines to alter time's flow, propelling us forward into the future or pulling us back into the past. While briefly captivated by this imagining, when the book or movie ends we still find ourselves decidedly in the present moment.

But that doesn't stop us from trying to turn back the clock. Lured by the desire to look younger, we mask the reminders of passing time with skin creams, hair coloring, and plastic surgery. Later, when old age is beyond disguise, we may begin to live in the past, retreating into a comforting world of old memories and wrapping ourselves in the golden days of youth.

There is such a deep desire within us to deny we're growing old.

Why are we so afraid? What are we so fearful of losing?

Journey to Midlife

A young boy throws a ball into the air, lofting it into endless blue sky. Each upward toss carries a dream of escaping gravity, of flying beyond treetops. But every time the ball slows to a stop, a small dot suspended in the sun's glare. Then it begins its inevitable tumble back into the boy's waiting hands.

Like the ball that flees gravity for a little while, the first part of life is fueled by youthful momentum. Relishing life's springtime, we acquire knowledge and skills as our future buds with promise, and we surge forward into the summer of life. Finally seasoned enough to be competent in our work, we are confident from weathering some life experiences, nourished by adult relationships, and perhaps enriched by our own family. We're measurably productive by worldly standards—we've acquired a house, perhaps some land, and paid vacation time—we savor the fruits of our hard work as we approach midlife.

But along with midlife come disturbing signs that we cannot ignore. Our teenager outdistances us while cycling; gray appears in our thinning hair; we can't stay up late anymore; it's harder to be fit. We overhear a new colleague—fresh from school—boast about being the innovative, cutting-edge addition to the company's over-the-hill team.

Like the ball tossed into the air, we reach the apex of our early life's upward journey. Physically, we slow down. Energy spent, we eventually stop at the top of the arc. Without forward momentum, we hang in midlife air.

Midlife Losses

Not used to stopping, we look around. What next?

The clock ticks.

In the past, we chose our destination, located it on the map of life, and worked diligently toward it. Adjusting our course along the way, we faced our limitations and let go of some of our dreams. By midlife, we reach the goals that are possible, only to experience a bewildering fatigue. Formerly energizing endeavors that gave meaning and purpose no longer interest us. Stalled in this midlife place, a friend muses, "I've worked hard all these years to reach many of my goals. Now what? Looking into the future, if I continue on this same path, it's blank. Nothing awaits me."

Momentarily suspended in the sun's glare, we hang between the known of our past and a dark unknown of our future. The compass that used to point the way now spins crazily. We're lost within the once-familiar landscape of our lives as our self-identity, carefully constructed these past decades, no longer means very much.

Who are we? What is important? Where are we going?

This puzzling, disorienting "slow-motion" stop can be agonizing. My medical school professor's words echo in the background. Even as we've climbed toward the sky, bursting to achieve, the clock has been ticking. We've been aging. At least half our lives—perhaps more—have already been lived.

The stillness at midlife's top of the arc is disturbing. Motionless, we're invited to let go of much that was important in the first part of life. We're also beckoned to face lingering fantasies and to let go of unrealistic dreams. In the silence, past decisions revisit us. A woman who chose not to have children says the irreversibility of menopause prompted her to revisit her earlier decision. Quieted, we ponder midlife's mystifying losses and wrestle with life-changing, foundation-shaking questions. In this slack-water place without tidal ebb and flow, there don't seem to be any obvious "next steps."

MEDICINE'S LOSS

"How can you sit here, eating lunch with me?" Esrom's lilting African voice, normally soft and gentle, rises to indignant strength. "In my country, people are dying for want of medical care. How can you not practice medicine?"

Esrom's hard question punctuates the quiet conversations around us in the seminary refectory, contrasting with discussions about theology, the rigors of translating Hebrew, and dynamics of parish life.

Most of us, including Esrom, are middle-aged and have left earlier careers. I mentally try on various replies. My practicing medicine in this country would not help people in your country. I have a sense of being "called" to ministry. I spent twenty-five years practicing medicine—isn't that enough? The replies are all true, but they're also defensive.

Perhaps, I think, there is no "answer." The silence grows, settling between us. I shake my head, shrug my shoulders, and smile a little.

Gentle again, he slowly nods and smiles back.

The geography of midlife is surreal. There's nothing "wrong" with us or the first part of our lives. In fact, our previous decades are absolutely vital parts of our journey and provide the foundation for the rest of our lives.

As a wide-eyed fourth grader, I want to be a doctor. I devour biographies of early women scientists and physicians and write school papers about them as they become part of my life. This momentum continues through college and propels me into medical school.

Practicing medicine is a privileged invitation into people's vulnerable lives. There are also sobering surprises. Emergency departments witness anger erupting into gun violence, drugs ruining despair-soaked lives, and ordinary mornings turning into grief-filled afternoons after which life is never the same. Over the years, my usual empathy tires as compassion fatigues. Shift work leaves me numb and bone-tired. Longtime emergency nurses admit to similar weariness. It's not that they don't care. It's that they cared so much and for so long that what caring room remains is reserved for extraordinary situations.

Esrom's question resounds.

Caught in midlife pause, I had less energy for medicine's changing climate—frivolous lawsuits and the escalating cost of care had radically altered the practice of medicine.

In the still of midlife I felt an invitation to a new look and a new listening. Just as that long-ago fourth grader who tended an injured rabbit knew cuddling was as important as a bandage, the seasoned physician understood that physical well-being was a mysterious mix of physical, psychological, and spiritual health. Pills do not treat underlying problems, and in midlife's landscape I realized that I couldn't just write prescriptions anymore. I took a deep breath and entered seminary.

What I cannot convey to Esrom over soup and cornbread is the ensuing midlife struggle—letting go of my previous life is a rocky, arduous journey. Anyone who takes a trip like this leaves behind decades of work, meaning, purpose, and identity. Even those of us who don't leave a previous career leave behind prior understandings and ways that we practiced our vocation.

To let go of our earlier self when a new self and future image does not yet exist is a strange loss. It's like swinging from one trapeze to another—we must let go of our trapeze and risk free-flight in the air before we can grasp the next trapeze. Until we let go of our past self and are willing to exist in midair, our next self cannot emerge. This journey through loss and aerial existence can take years.

Midlife Gifts

The gifts of midlife are very different from earlier gifts. We do not choose them, plot a course, and work to obtain them. Rather they are true gifts—pure, unexpected, and unearned. Consider these astonishing presents:

Freedom

Even the most uncomfortable, disorienting midlife pause bestows the gift of freedom. Liberated from our earlier all-consuming trajectory, we are free to explore new territory and discover new possibilities we were too busy for in the past.

Openness

The last thing my parents taught me was how to die. Paradoxically, they also taught me how to live. I hear the clock ticking in my life. Invited to look without blinking into reality, I see there's not much time left; mine is the next generation to die. This unflinching gaze bestows the gift of a heady openness to all that could be. Having less time left bequeaths a wondrously heightened appreciation of every moment. Each day is a treasured gift.

Exploration

The desires and talents we suppressed earlier because they didn't serve our single-minded purpose can now come gently forth. We discover the delight of nurturing these unused, hidden parts of who we are. We can finally learn to play the piano or to paint. We can volunteer at the homeless shelter or tutor children after school. We can work for environmental causes or speak out for human rights. This part of life becomes a "yes" as we encounter and embrace a newfound wholeness of our astonishing selves.

Now that the demands of life's first part no longer determine who we are, we see with extended vision and learn to interweave aspects of life we previously held separate. Boundaries soften between earlier choices: am I a physician *or* a beginning art student? Now we realize we can embrace both. As our occupation no longer dominates our priorities, relationships assume more importance. Given a second chance at parenting, previously hard-hitting career men become gentle grandpas as they relish their playful grandbabies.

Midlife gives birth to the autumn of our lives. Once we let go of life's first part, the delightful crispness of these fall mornings bestows new clarity. Astonishingly, this season has the rich pleasures of a lingering Indian summer with a bountiful crop of autumn gifts. We're invited to indulge.

The Losses of Aging

When we look down from midlife's arc, it seems that a long, earthbound free fall awaits us. The arc of the ball that the boy tossed into the air marks the path of our physical aging.

Growing old entails an alarming passivity of letting gravity pull us downward as life reverses polarity in a stomach-in-your-throat plummet. We travel back the way we came, only this time in the opposite direction and on vastly different terms. In this free fall, we let go of what we previously acquired as we lose the ability to walk, to see, to hear, to think clearly, and to interact with the rapidly changing world. We learn to live with chronic pain and become dependent on pills to bolster failing organs. Each year brings further physical deterioration and more limitations. While we can't unwind time, this seems like an unwinding of much of the first part of our lives.

These losses are radically different from the losses in our first part of life. We now lose things we haven't outgrown—things we need to sustain our lives. These losses are irreversible and cumulative and will continue until we have physically lost so much that our bodies cannot live. Grief, an occasional visitor in the first part of life, now moves in and becomes a companion.

Invited to enter a place we'd never choose, we travel far from our earlier denial. In *Aging as a Spiritual Journey,* Eugene Bianchi, a specialist on the spirituality of aging, bluntly states that we must "enter the experience of the sands slipping away in the hourglass of our lives. This discomforting feeling of the unstoppable dimming of the light, the numbering of our breaths, must be embraced until it hurts."[1]

My father never lost his outrage at having to relinquish his driver's license—mere mention of this loss evoked powerful emotions and words from this mild, gentle man as he raged against his doctor and the state. For this loss signaled much deeper losses and was the harbinger of my parents' most grievous loss—the ability to live independently in the home they built and in which they raised their children.

Our culture ties our sense of worth to our independence. As we grow more reliant on others, we must look deeper to unmask a more profound self-identity. Who are we now that we do not plan our days and drive to our appointments, now that we can't prepare our own meals or balance our checkbooks? Who are we now that we've given up our privacy as we're helped to dress, take our pills, and get to the doctor? Our true identity is not defined by our culture, and we must venture far from society's norms in search of ourselves.

Midlife's search to uncover our more profound identity, to embrace a newfound wholeness, was good practice as we learned our sense of self was not defined by our previous accomplishments or acquisitions. Now, as old age advances, we are beckoned to discover our most profound identity, which is remarkably untethered to culture's obsession with youth, independence, or productivity. Old age unmasks wisdom we have feared to confront our entire life.

With startling clarity, we now see that we've never been self-sufficient at any time in our lives. We've always depended upon others for our existence. Our sense of autonomous existence, our sense of control, were mere illusions.

> *The backdoor to Catherine's cottage is past daffodils and uneven spring grass. Oddly shaped glass bottles decorate the windowsill, breakfast dishes are in the sink and left-over egg in the skillet as I enter through the kitchen. Catherine lies on a sofa bed in the living room.*
>
> *Her daughters cluster around as I pull up a low stool alongside Catherine's bed. "I was so disappointed this morning," Catherine whispers. "Last night I said good-bye to the daffodils. I knew it was my last night. But then I opened my eyes this morning—and saw daffodils. I'm still here," Catherine sighs. "There must be one more conversation I'm supposed to have."*

Catherine has played her last piece on her harp and said good-bye to her daughters and close friends. She is ready for death, walking into the experience as she's walked through her fully lived life. She's been prepared to die since she made her decision to forgo treatment for cancer. Several months ago she informed her daughters that she had lived an extraordinary and blessed life and was now dying. She invited them to travel these last days together. An artist, Catherine walked her own unique journey through living, and now through dying.

Bedridden and completely dependent, Catherine taught profound lessons. She had always modeled for her daughters how to risk seeing every daffodil and every day as astounding gifts. And now in her acceptance of letting go of it all, she received and shared the gift of dying with us. Even in her acceptance of death's disappointing timing, she continued to perceive the gift of one last important conversation.

The Gift of Wisdom

To grow old is to live a paradox. New life does emerge out of the ashes of our losses, sometimes with the dazzling colors of the phoenix. A larger wisdom gently settles on us, which sees beyond previous horizons and past old boundaries.

We have no choice in the wintertime losses of our lives, but we can choose our response to them. In our fear-filled gaze into the free fall of aging, we see only the negative at first. We're terrified of blue veins that crisscross our tissue-thin skin, a shuffling walker-assisted gait, and incontinence. These are surely grievous physical losses. But from earlier experience, we've learned to look unflinchingly in the mirror, name and mourn the relentless march of losses, and then let them go.

The clock ticks so loudly that sometimes we can hear little else.

As much as my father feared assisted living, once there, he discovered some unexpected gifts. There was enjoyable social interaction, an exercise program he rarely missed, music and church services, better food than he could ever cook, and transportation to concerts and on day trips. He still grieved the loss of his house and his driver's license, but by finally letting them go, he regained some sense of control and decision making about his days—diminished to be sure, but still present.

Accepting our limitations can paradoxically free us. When we've no longer anything to acquire, grasp, or control, our open hands can receive gifts. People who age compassionately tell me that their continual low-level grief lets them accept the ceaseless losses and leads them to a surprising gratitude for what is left. The simplest act of appreciating a flower outside the window brings immeasurable delight. We can stare once again at creation in toddlerlike wonder. Though our knees will not let us physically kneel, deep inside we kneel in gratitude for each day's small, wondrous pleasures.

We've never had to let go of so much. Our diminishment cuts deep as we become increasingly vulnerable. And yet, this too is womb-space.

Although we'd never choose it, this place and these years can birth a wholeness we've never before known.

In early gestation, who would have thought that eventually leaving our first womb would be a good idea? As a toddler or a middle schooler, who would have envisioned leaving our childhood home as helpful? As a young adult, would we have dreamed that letting go of our single-minded focus and incessant energy to acquire could be essential? And in midlife's pause and autumn's physical decline, could we ever have embraced the winter of our lives as womb-space giving birth yet again to the deepest layers of our self?

All birth—including this birth of wisdom—entails loss. Will we completely lose ourselves in this birth? Can we suffer the anguish of this monumental letting go and dying to enable—yet again—another borning? In our frailty, can we let go of the trapeze and exist in midair before seeing the next trapeze?

Completely unattached from our achieving self, culture's norms, and our own expectations, the work of our last years is a profound and liberating journey to follow where the spirit takes us. As we let go of so much in old age, we painfully shuffle into life's ultimate paradox. After we've lost nearly everything, we finally grow into the complete person God created us to be.

What began with midlife's intoxicating embrace of long-suppressed gifts and talents now proceeds to an even deeper level of wholeness as we're finally mature enough to embrace the shadow part of ourselves that we previously denied. This is the ultimate disillusionment, the difficult gift of our lifelong relationship with living and loving and letting go. The poet Rumi invites us to welcome the darker pieces of our self when they visit and to invite them in. He suggests we be grateful for these shadow traits as they are "guides" that teach us many things.

This is the sacred ground of healing and wholeness. Our aging body teaches us how to ultimately let go of all the interior things we've clutched for so long. As our body deteriorates, we're invited to detach from anger and self-righteousness, fear and denial, pride and pretense that hide our vulnerability. These are our last days to let go of bitterness, to forgive the past, and to be made whole. Our old wounds and painful memories can finally heal as we see the past anew.

Compassion springs forth when we embrace our shadows and regrets, accepting the totality of ourselves with gentleness and love. Now we can also love others and their shadowy sides with a freedom we've never known and a compassion we've never experienced.

If we do not accept this invitation—if we continue to deny the difficult parts of ourselves—we miss the gift of grace-filled flexibility that can come with aging. If we choose to not name, mourn, and let go of our losses, they molder inside. Our fear, displeasure, and disgust for those aspects of ourselves and our past lives erupt outward to poison others. We become stiff and unbending, endlessly complaining, and vainly trying to control the uncontrollable.

Gray hair comes with a price as well as a gift. We've experienced so many losses in our lives. We know that winter—even this winter of our last years—can turn into spring unlike any we've ever experienced, a springtime budding of ourselves that couldn't have happened until now. Unexpectedly, there can be an exquisite wisdom-flowering in this seemingly stark and barren winter of life.

At the Benedictine monastery of Christ in the Desert, I kneel with black-robed monks at Compline, the last prayer of the day. In the desert's great silence after prayer, the beauty of day's end is arresting. The sun paints the desert floor and mesa cliffs in glorious colors. I walk and wonder as the sun now begins to set on the arc of my life's journey: "Are my last days also painted in glorious color? Is there brilliance in these last years as I walk into my life's evening and night, as I enter life's great silence?" If only I may have eyes to see.

Perhaps in these days, the sacred love in which we are created flames its brightest, lighting up the darkness of our failing vision and this last, long winter night. We learn to see by a different light now, one that isn't so earthbound and dependent on our physical state. Perhaps we begin to live more from our "created in the image of God" center. Our frail bodies and wrinkled skin, our brittle bones and rheumy eyes belie the deep beauty and burning fire that cannot be housed in a youthful body.

"There is a time to be born, and a time to die ..."

As we approach our true home from whence we came, we learn to see that we've always been home. Our physical birth just seemed to separate us from each other and from God. But the truth is we never left home at all. The sacred depths of love, both human and divine, let us glimpse this truth. The persistent cycle of life's losses and gifts pulls us into deeper understandings of what lies beneath surface reality. Until now, we couldn't see as clearly. Now we know.

Coyote's howl and a little girl's voice call for something we have never lost.

Spiritual Practice
GUIDED MEDITATION

A guided meditation can lead us to interact with a scripture passage in a deep, personal way. Questions invite us to walk into the passage, to imaginatively be a part of the scripture, to let scripture words speak their wisdom or challenge or healing into our lives. This is a prayerful listening for what scripture has to say to us this day, at this moment.

- Find a quiet prayer place. Hold people and concerns of the day in prayer, then release them to God. Take a long, slow breath. Relax your body. Settle into awareness of your breathing or into a breath prayer.

- When quieted, very slowly read the following scripture from the gospel of John. Take your time and let each phrase sink into you.

> *Very truly, I tell you, when you were younger,*
> *you used to fasten your own belt and go*
> > *wherever you wished.*
> *But when you grow old,*
> *you will stretch out your hands,*
> *and someone else will fasten a belt around you*
> *and take you where you do not wish to go.*
> > > *John 21:18*

- When you are quieted, read the same scripture phrase by phrase as printed on the next page. Let your God-given imagination carry you back in time to when you were young and forward in time to when you will be old. Pause after each question to leisurely ponder and play with it. Let memories, thoughts and emotions flow freely—even those you might wish to suppress.

I tell you, when you were younger,

Imagine being young again.
   How do you look?
   How do you feel?
   What do you wear?
   Where do you live?

you used to fasten your own belt and go
   wherever you wished.

   As your youthful self, what do you love to do?
   Where do you love to go?
   What do you delight in doing well—
   those activities in which you "fasten your
      own belt"?

But when you grow old,

   Let images of growing old freely come to mind.
   Who do you know who is elderly? How do
      they look?
   Describe them. What happens to bodies as
      they age?
   What signs of aging does your body have?
   Imagine yourself when you are old.
   How do you look?
   How do you feel?

you will stretch out your hands,

   As an elderly adult, for what do you stretch
      out your hands?
   For what do you yearn?
   To whom do you stretch your hands?
   For whom do you long?

*and someone else will fasten a belt around you
and take you where you do not wish to go.*

> *Where on this journey of aging do you not
>   wish to go?*
> *What do you most fear? What other fears do
>   you have?*

> *For what are you grateful?*

> *Let your thoughts, memories, emotions settle.*
> *Take a deep breath. Rest in God's presence.*

Personal journeys into scripture can be powerful. Over the next days, more images, emotions, and thoughts may surface. Fresh insights can come long after the meditation. You may wish to revisit the scripture. It is fruitful to spend prayerful time with whatever arises after the meditation.

Exploring Deeper

Journey of Aging

- Seek out a quiet place. Recall your current joys and concerns, your unfinished tasks. Hold them in your thoughts for a moment and then let them go. Take a deep breath. Settle into this space.
- Remember the first decades of your life leading to midlife. What excited you and where did you spend your energy?
- What did you acquire? Recall the skills and competencies, experiences and degrees, jobs and material possessions you acquired. What about personal and family commitments?
- Have you experienced midlife's stillness, lack of forward momentum? Did you lose energy for what previously gave you purpose and meaning?

- What were your thoughts and emotions?
- What were your losses? What were the gifts?
- If you have passed through midlife into old age, what losses have you experienced? What gifts have you received?
- What losses do you most fear about old age? What gifts might there be?

Pray

Where can I go from your spirit?
Or where can I flee from your presence?
If I ascend to heaven, you are there;
if I make my bed in Sheol, you are there.
If I take the wings of the morning
and settle at the farthest limits of the sea,
even there your hand shall lead me,
and your right hand shall hold me fast.

                                  Psalm 139:7–10

Epilogue

My mountain maple is now full with summer's leafy abundance. The writing of this book has taken me on a journey from autumn's lonely leaf-fall through winter's stark barrenness and spring's new growth. Another year has passed, as creation once again has taught me profound lessons of loss, death, and new birth.

My mother, father, and Colin are close today as I write a funeral service for a beloved woman whose family is now embarking on a long journey through the valley of loss and grief. They will be forever changed by this travel, but abundance outside reminds me that in due time, their grief will open out into summer's new life.

The rhythm of gift and loss that begins with our birth and overarches our lives until our last breath has ended for this woman. But her family—and you and I, too—still live immersed in this endless flow. Along the way, we learn that for anything new to be born, something must die. Life can be walked with gently cupped hands that allow us to let go of outgrown or passing gifts and to receive new ones. There is an art to holding the things of life loosely, letting them flow into and out of our lives without painful grasping. Even our long-term relationships continually require us to let go to enable growth and new ways of relating. Again and again, like the repeating cycles of passing seasons, we learn to let go. And in the loss, we receive new gifts.

Funerals bring us face to face with our most painful losses, as our God-given ability to love measures our grief. Funerals call us to name our agonizing losses and to fully travel the stark winter of grief. They expose our underlying sense of yearning, of divine homesickness; they amplify the ache in our everyday lives. Coyotes howl in the night, and we cry for those we mourn. We seem so very far from home.

It seems incomprehensible at the time, but in our deepest loss, as we let go of the physical presence of our loved ones and reweave them into our lives anew, daffodils continue to bloom, people still love us, rain falls, and everyday gifts are still given. The barrenness of grief may forever distance us from the "god" of platitudes, easy faith, quick answers, and human certainty. But God—whose name is "I am," who appears in Mt. Sinai cloud, who in the dark of night empties tombs—is very present in the shadowy valleys of loss.

At the funeral this afternoon, we will celebrate, fully savor, and give thanks to God for the gift of this well-loved woman. I will remind the congregation that my African friends call funerals homecomings. For there is indeed a sense of coming home in the passing of a wife-mother-grandmother-friend whom we all mourn. But there is also a glimpse of homecoming for us. As full of hope as the young faces of her grandchildren, somewhere in these passages through loss the clouds drift apart for a moment, and we too hear echoes of sacred home and presence, which may not be so very far away at all.

> O LORD, you have searched me and known me.
> You know when I sit down and when I rise up;
> you discern my thoughts from far away.
> You search out my path and my lying down,
> and are acquainted with all my ways.
> Even before a word is on my tongue,
> O LORD, you know it completely.
> You hem me in, behind and before,
> and lay your hand upon me.
>
> *Psalm 139:1–5*

Notes

1. The Human Tapestry

1. Barbara Brown Taylor, *The Preaching Life* (Boston: Cowley, 1993), 13.
2. Robert Neimeyer, ed., *Meaning Reconstruction and the Experience of Loss* (Washington, DC: American Psychological Association, 2001), 36.
3. Marcus Borg, *The Heart of Christianity* (New York: HarperCollins, 2003), 113–114.

2. Birth Pangs and Passages

1. Christina Feldman and Jack Kornfield, eds., *Stories of the Spirit, Stories of the Heart: Parables of Spiritual Faith from Around the World* (New York: HarperCollins, 1991).
2. Margaret Mahler, *The Psychological Birth of the Human Infant: Symbiosis and Individuation* (New York: Basic Books, 1975), 3.
3. Kenneth Mitchell and Herbert Anderson, *All Our Losses, All Our Griefs: Resources for Pastoral Care* (Louisville: Westminster John Knox Press, 1983), 51.
4. Thich Nhat Hanh, *The Long Road Turns to Joy: A Guide to Walking Meditation* (Berkeley: Parallax Press, 1996), 5.

4. Things and Places

1. J.R.R. Tolkein, *The Two Towers* (Boston: Houghton Mifflin, 1954), 220.

5. The Ebb and Flow of Relationships

1. *Book of Common Worship* (Louisville: Westminster John Knox Press, 1993), 845.

6. Relationships That Unravel and Tear Apart

1. Pauline Boss, *Ambiguous Loss: Learning to Live with Unresolved Grief* (Cambridge: Harvard University Press, 1999), 8.

2. Ann Weems, *Psalms of Lament* (Louisville: Westminster John Knox Press, 1995), xv.

3. C. S. Lewis, *A Grief Observed* (New York: HarperCollins, 1989), 60.

7. When Foundations Shake and Crumble

1. Kieran Kavanaugh and Otilio Rodrieguez, trans. and eds., *The Collected Works of St John of the Cross* (Washington, DC: ICS Publications, 1973), 163.

2. Brian Kolodiejchuk, ed., *Come Be My Light* (New York: Doubleday, 2007), 210.

3. Timothy Fry, ed., *The Rule of St Benedict in Latin and English with Notes* (Collegeville, MN: Liturgical Press, 1981), 157.

8. The Passing of Time: Our Final Loss … and Gift

1. Eugene Bianchi, *Aging as a Spiritual Journey* (New York: Crossroad, 1982), 16.

Suggestions for Further Reading

Brennan, Anne, and Janice Brewi. *Passion for Life: Lifelong Psychological and Spiritual Growth*. New York: Continuum International Publishing Group, 1999.

Edwards, Tilden. *Living in the Presence: Spiritual Exercises to Open Our Lives to the Awareness of God*. San Francisco: HarperSanFrancisco, 1995.

Fischer, Kathleen. *Winter Grace: Spirituality and Aging*. Nashville: Upper Room Books, 1998.

Ford, Marcia. *Finding Hope: Cultivating God's Gift of a Hopeful Spirit*. Woodstock, VT: SkyLight Paths, 2006.

Marshall, Jay. *Thanking & Blessing—The Sacred Art: Spiritual Vitality through Gratefulness*. Woodstock, VT: SkyLight Paths, 2007.

May, Gerald G. *The Dark Night of the Soul: A Psychiatrist Explores the Connection between Darkness and Spiritual Growth*. San Francisco: HarperSanFrancisco, 2004.

Mitchell, Kenneth, and Herbert Anderson. *All Our Losses, All Our Griefs: Resources for Pastoral Care*. Louisville: Westminster John Knox Press, 1983.

Neimeyer, Robert A. *Meaning Reconstruction and the Experience of Loss*. Washington, DC: American Psychological Association, 2001.

Peerman, Gordon. *Blessed Relief: What Christians Can Learn from Buddhists about Suffering*. Woodstock, VT: SkyLight Paths, 2008.

Spitz, Elie Kaplan. *Healing from Despair: Choosing Wholeness in a Broken World*. With Erica Shapiro Taylor. Woodstock, VT: Jewish Lights, 2008.

Taylor, Terry. *A Spirituality for Brokenness: Discovering Your Deepest Self in Difficult Times*. Woodstock, VT: SkyLight Paths, 2009.

Viorst, Judith. *Necessary Losses*. New York: The Free Press, 1986.

Weems, Ann. *Psalms of Lament*. Louisville: Westminster John Knox Press, 1995.

AVAILABLE FROM BETTER BOOKSTORES.
TRY YOUR BOOKSTORE FIRST.

Global Spiritual Perspectives

Spiritual Perspectives on America's Role as Superpower
by the Editors at SkyLight Paths
Are we the world's good neighbor or a global bully? From a spiritual perspective, what are America's responsibilities as the only remaining superpower? Contributors:
Dr. Beatrice Bruteau • Dr. Joan Brown Campbell • Tony Campolo • Rev. Forrest Church • Lama Surya Das • Matthew Fox • Kabir Helminski • Thich Nhat Hanh • Eboo Patel • Abbot M. Basil Pennington, ocso • Dennis Prager • Rosemary Radford Ruether • Wayne Teasdale • Rev. William McD. Tully • Rabbi Arthur Waskow • John Wilson
5½ x 8½, 256 pp, Quality PB, 978-1-893361-81-2 **$16.95**

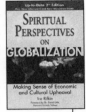

Spiritual Perspectives on Globalization, 2nd Edition
Making Sense of Economic and Cultural Upheaval
by Ira Rifkin; Foreword by Dr. David Little, Harvard Divinity School
What is globalization? Surveys the religious landscape. Includes a new Discussion Guide designed for group use.
5½ x 8½, 256 pp, Quality PB, 978-1-59473-045-0 **$16.99**

Hinduism / Vedanta

The Four Yogas
A Guide to the Spiritual Paths of Action, Devotion, Meditation and Knowledge
by Swami Adiswarananda
6 x 9, 320 pp, Quality PB, 978-1-59473-223-2 **$19.99**; HC, 978-1-59473-143-3 **$29.99**

Meditation & Its Practices
A Definitive Guide to Techniques and Traditions of Meditation in Yoga and Vedanta
by Swami Adiswarananda 6 x 9, 504 pp, Quality PB, 978-1-59473-105-1 **$24.99**

The Spiritual Quest and the Way of Yoga: The Goal, the Journey and the Milestones
by Swami Adiswarananda 6 x 9, 288 pp, HC, 978-1-59473-113-6 **$29.99**

Sri Ramakrishna, the Face of Silence
by Swami Nikhilananda and Dhan Gopal Mukerji
Edited with an Introduction by Swami Adiswarananda; Foreword by Dhan Gopal Mukerji II
Classic biographies present the life and thought of Sri Ramakrishna.
6 x 9, 352 pp, Quality PB, 978-1-59473-233-1 **$21.99**; HC, 978-1-59473-115-0 **$29.99**

Sri Sarada Devi, The Holy Mother: Her Teachings and Conversations
Translated with Notes by Swami Nikhilananda; Edited with an Introduction by Swami Adiswarananda
6 x 9, 288 pp, HC, 978-1-59473-070-2 **$29.99**

The Vedanta Way to Peace and Happiness *by Swami Adiswarananda*
6 x 9, 240 pp, Quality PB, 978-1-59473-180-8 **$18.99**

Vivekananda, World Teacher: His Teachings on the Spiritual Unity of Humankind
Edited and with an Introduction by Swami Adiswarananda
6 x 9, 272 pp, Quality PB, 978-1-59473-210-2 **$21.99**

Sikhism

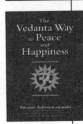

The First Sikh Spiritual Master
Timeless Wisdom from the Life and Teachings of Guru Nanak *by Harish Dhillon*
Tells the story of a unique spiritual leader who showed a gentle, peaceful path to God-realization while highlighting Guru Nanak's quest for tolerance and compassion. 6 x 9, 192 pp, Quality PB, 978-1-59473-209-6 **$16.99**

Or phone, fax, mail or e-mail to: **SKYLIGHT PATHS** Publishing
Sunset Farm Offices, Route 4 • P.O. Box 237 • Woodstock, Vermont 05091
Tel: (802) 457-4000 • Fax: (802) 457-4004 • www.skylightpaths.com
Credit card orders: (800) 962-4544 (8:30AM–5:30PM ET Monday–Friday)
Generous discounts on quantity orders. SATISFACTION GUARANTEED. Prices subject to change.

Children's Spirituality

ENDORSED BY CATHOLIC, PROTESTANT, JEWISH, AND BUDDHIST RELIGIOUS LEADERS

Adam and Eve's First Sunset: God's New Day
by Sandy Eisenberg Sasso; Full-color illus. by Joani Keller Rothenberg 9 x 12, 32 pp, Full-color illus., HC, 978-1-58023-177-0 **$17.95** *For ages 4 & up (A book from Jewish Lights, SkyLight Paths' sister imprint)*

Because Nothing Looks Like God
by Lawrence and Karen Kushner; Full-color illus. by Dawn W. Majewski
Real-life examples of happiness and sadness introduce children to the possibilities of spiritual life. 11 x 8½, 32 pp, HC, Full-color illus., 978-1-58023-092-6 **$17.99** *For ages 4 & up (A book from Jewish Lights, SkyLight Paths' sister imprint)*
Also available: **Teacher's Guide**, 8½ x 11, 22 pp, PB, 978-1-58023-140-4 **$6.95** *For ages 5–8*

But God Remembered: Stories of Women from Creation to the Promised Land
by Sandy Eisenberg Sasso; Full-color illus. by Bethanne Andersen
A fascinating collection of four different stories of women only briefly mentioned in biblical tradition and religious texts.
9 x 12, 32 pp, Full-color illus., Quality PB, 978-1-58023-372-9 **$12.99**; HC, 978-1-879045-43-9 **$16.95**
For ages 8 & up (A book from Jewish Lights, SkyLight Paths' sister imprint)

Cain & Abel: Finding the Fruits of Peace
by Sandy Eisenberg Sasso; Full-color illus. by Joani Keller Rothenberg
A sensitive recasting of the ancient tale shows we have the power to deal with anger in positive ways. "Editor's Choice"—American Library Association's *Booklist*
9 x 12, 32 pp, HC, Full-color illus., 978-1-58023-123-7 **$16.95** *For ages 5 & up (A book from Jewish Lights, SkyLight Paths' sister imprint)*

Does God Hear My Prayer?
by August Gold; Full-color photos by Diane Hardy Waller
Introduces preschoolers and young readers to prayer and how it helps them express their own emotions. 10 x 8½, 32 pp, Quality PB, Full-color photo illus., 978-1-59473-102-0 **$8.99**

The 11th Commandment: Wisdom from Our Children *by The Children of America*
"If there were an Eleventh Commandment, what would it be?" Children of many religious denominations across America answer this question—in their own drawings and words. "A rare book of spiritual celebration for all people, of all ages, for all time." —*Bookviews* 8 x 10, 48 pp, HC, Full-color illus., 978-1-879045-46-0 **$16.95**
For all ages (A book from Jewish Lights, SkyLight Paths' sister imprint)

For Heaven's Sake *by Sandy Eisenberg Sasso; Full-color illus. by Kathryn Kunz Finney*
What heaven is and where to find it. 9 x 12, 32 pp, HC, Full-color illus., 978-1-58023-054-4 **$16.95** *For ages 4 & up (A book from Jewish Lights, SkyLight Paths' sister imprint)*

God in Between *by Sandy Eisenberg Sasso; Full-color illus. by Sally Sweetland*
A magical, mythical tale that teaches that God can be found where we are.
9 x 12, 32 pp, HC, Full-color illus., 978-1-879045-86-6 **$16.95** *For ages 4 & up (A book from Jewish Lights, SkyLight Paths' sister imprint)*

God's Paintbrush: Special 10th Anniversary Edition
Invites children of all faiths and backgrounds to encounter God through moments in their own lives. 11 x 8½, 32 pp, Full-color illus., HC, 978-1-58023-195-4 **$17.95** *For ages 4 & up*
Also available: **I Am God's Paintbrush** (A Board Book)
by Sandy Eisenberg Sasso; Full-color illus. by Annette Compton
5 x 5, 24 pp, Board Book, Full-color illus., 978-1-59473-265-2 **$7.99** *For ages 0–4*
Also available: **God's Paintbrush Teacher's Guide** 8½ x 11, 32 pp, PB, 978-1-879045-57-6 **$8.95**

God's Paintbrush Celebration Kit
A Spiritual Activity Kit for Teachers and Students of All Faiths, All Backgrounds
Additional activity sheets available:
8-Student Activity Sheet Pack (40 sheets/5 sessions), 978-1-58023-058-2 **$19.95**
Single-Student Activity Sheet Pack (5 sessions), 978-1-58023-059-9 **$3.95**

Children's Spirituality

ENDORSED BY CATHOLIC, PROTESTANT, JEWISH, AND BUDDHIST RELIGIOUS LEADERS

Remembering My Grandparent: A Kid's Own Grief Workbook in the Christian Tradition *by Nechama Liss-Levinson, PhD, and Rev. Molly Phinney Baskette, MDiv* 8 x 10, 48 pp, 2-color text, HC, 978-1-59473-212-6 **$16.99** *For ages 7–13*

Does God Ever Sleep? *by Joan Sauro, CSJ; Full-color photos*
A charming nighttime reminder that God is always present in our lives.
10 x 8½, 32 pp, Quality PB, Full-color photos, 978-1-59473-110-5 **$8.99** *For ages 3–6*

Does God Forgive Me? *by August Gold; Full-color photos by Diane Hardy Waller*
Gently shows how God forgives all that we do if we are truly sorry.
10 x 8½, 32 pp, Quality PB, Full-color photos, 978-1-59473-142-6 **$8.99** *For ages 3–6*

God Said Amen *by Sandy Eisenberg Sasso; Full-color illus. by Avi Katz*
A warm and inspiring tale of two kingdoms that shows us that we need only reach out to each other to find the answers to our prayers.
9 x 12, 32 pp, HC, Full-color illus., 978-1-58023-080-3 **$16.95**
For ages 4 & up (A book from Jewish Lights, SkyLight Paths' sister imprint)

How Does God Listen? *by Kay Lindahl; Full-color photos by Cynthia Maloney*
How do we know when God is listening to us? Children will find the answers to these questions as they engage their senses while the story unfolds, learning how God listens in the wind, waves, clouds, hot chocolate, perfume, our tears and our laughter.
10 x 8½, 32 pp, Quality PB, Full-color photos, 978-1-59473-084-9 **$8.99** *For ages 3–6*

In God's Hands *by Lawrence Kushner and Gary Schmidt; Full-color illus. by Matthew J. Baeck*
9 x 12, 32 pp, Full-color illus., HC, 978-1-58023-224-1 **$16.99** *For ages 5 & up (A book from Jewish Lights, SkyLight Paths' sister imprint)*

In God's Name *by Sandy Eisenberg Sasso; Full-color illus. by Phoebe Stone*
Like an ancient myth in its poetic text and vibrant illustrations, this award-winning modern fable about the search for God's name celebrates the diversity and, at the same time, the unity of all the people of the world.
9 x 12, 32 pp, HC, Full-color illus., 978-1-879045-26-2 **$16.99**
For ages 4 & up (A book from Jewish Lights, SkyLight Paths' sister imprint)

Also available in Spanish: **El nombre de Dios**
9 x 12, 32 pp, HC, Full-color illus., 978-1-893361-63-8 **$16.95**

In Our Image: God's First Creatures
by Nancy Sohn Swartz; Full-color illus. by Melanie Hall
A playful new twist on the Genesis story—from the perspective of the animals. Celebrates the interconnectedness of nature and the harmony of all living things.
9 x 12, 32 pp, HC, Full-color illus., 978-1-879045-99-6 **$16.95**
For ages 4 & up (A book from Jewish Lights, SkyLight Paths' sister imprint)

Noah's Wife: The Story of Naamah
by Sandy Eisenberg Sasso; Full-color illus. by Bethanne Andersen
This new story, based on an ancient text, opens readers' religious imaginations to new ideas about the well-known story of the Flood. When God tells Noah to bring the animals of the world onto the ark, God also calls on Naamah, Noah's wife, to save each plant on Earth.
9 x 12, 32 pp, HC, Full-color illus., 978-1-58023-134-3 **$16.95**
For ages 4 & up (A book from Jewish Lights, SkyLight Paths' sister imprint)

Also available: **Naamah:** Noah's Wife (A Board Book)
by Sandy Eisenberg Sasso; Full-color illus. by Bethanne Andersen
5 x 5, 24 pp, Board Book, Full-color illus., 978-1-893361-56-0 **$7.99** *For ages 0–4*

Where Does God Live? *by August Gold and Matthew J. Perlman*
Using simple, everyday examples that children can relate to, this colorful book helps young readers develop a personal understanding of God.
10 x 8½, 32 pp, Quality PB, Full-color photo illus., 978-1-893361-39-3 **$8.99** *For ages 3–6*

Children's Spirituality—Board Books

Adam and Eve's New Day (A Board Book)
by Sandy Eisenberg Sasso; Full-color illus. by Joani Keller Rothenberg
A lesson in hope for every child who has worried about what comes next. Abridged from *Adam and Eve's First Sunset*.
5 x 5, 24 pp, Full-color illus., Board Book, 978-1-59473-205-8 **$7.99** *For ages 0–4*

How Did the Animals Help God? (A Board Book)
by Nancy Sohn Swartz; Full-color illus. by Melanie Hall
Abridged from *In Our Image*, God asks all of nature to offer gifts to humankind—with a promise that they will care for creation in return.
5 x 5, 24 pp, Board Book, Full-color illus., 978-1-59473-044-3 **$7.99** *For ages 0–4*

Where Is God? (A Board Book) *by Lawrence and Karen Kushner; Full-color illus. by Dawn W. Majewski* A gentle way for young children to explore how God is with us every day, in every way. Abridged from *Because Nothing Looks Like God*.
5 x 5, 24 pp, Board Book, Full-color illus., 978-1-893361-17-1 **$7.99** *For ages 0–4*

What Does God Look Like? (A Board Book)
by Lawrence and Karen Kushner; Full-color illus. by Dawn W. Majewski
A simple way for young children to explore the ways that we "see" God. Abridged from *Because Nothing Looks Like God*.
5 x 5, 24 pp, Board Book, Full-color illus., 978-1-893361-23-2 **$7.99** *For ages 0–4*

How Does God Make Things Happen? (A Board Book)
by Lawrence and Karen Kushner; Full-color illus. by Dawn W. Majewski
A charming invitation for young children to explore how God makes things happen in our world. Abridged from *Because Nothing Looks Like God*.
5 x 5, 24 pp, Board Book, Full-color illus., 978-1-893361-24-9 **$7.99** *For ages 0–4*

What Is God's Name? (A Board Book)
by Sandy Eisenberg Sasso; Full-color illus. by Phoebe Stone
Everyone and everything in the world has a name. What is God's name? Abridged from the award-winning *In God's Name*.
5 x 5, 24 pp, Board Book, Full-color illus., 978-1-893361-10-2 **$7.99** *For ages 0–4*

What You Will See Inside ...

This important new series of books, each with many full-color photos, is designed to show children ages 6 and up the Who, What, When, Where, Why and How of traditional houses of worship, liturgical celebrations, and rituals of different world faiths, empowering them to respect and understand their own religious traditions—and those of their friends and neighbors.

What You Will See Inside a Catholic Church
by Reverend Michael Keane; Foreword by Robert J. Keeley, EdD
Full-color photos by Aaron Pepis
8½ x 10½, 32 pp, Full-color photos, HC, 978-1-893361-54-6 **$17.95**

Also available in Spanish: **Lo que se puede ver dentro de una iglesia católica**
8½ x 10½, 32 pp, Full-color photos, HC, 978-1-893361-66-9 **$16.95**

What You Will See Inside a Hindu Temple
by Dr. Mahendra Jani and Dr. Vandana Jani; Full-color photos by Neirah Bhargava and Vijay Dave
8½ x 10½, 32 pp, Full-color photos, HC, 978-1-59473-116-7 **$17.99**

What You Will See Inside a Mosque
by Aisha Karen Khan; Full-color photos by Aaron Pepis
8½ x 10½, 32 pp, Full-color photos, Quality PB, 978-1-59473-257-7 **$12.99**; HC, 978-1-893361-60-7 **$16.95**

What You Will See Inside a Synagogue
by Rabbi Lawrence A. Hoffman and Dr. Ron Wolfson; Full-color photos by Bill Aron
8½ x 10½, 32 pp, Full-color photos, Quality PB, 978-1-59473-256-0 **$12.99**; HC, 978-1-59473-012-2 **$17.99**

Children's Spiritual Biography

Ten Amazing People
And How They Changed the World
by Maura D. Shaw; Foreword by Dr. Robert Coles
Full-color illus. by Stephen Marchesi

For ages 7 & up

Black Elk • Dorothy Day • Malcolm X • Mahatma Gandhi • Martin Luther King, Jr. • Mother Teresa • Janusz Korczak • Desmond Tutu • Thich Nhat Hanh • Albert Schweitzer

This vivid, inspirational and authoritative book will open new possibilities for children by telling the stories of how ten of the past century's greatest leaders changed the world in important ways.
8½ x 11, 48 pp, HC, Full-color illus., 978-1-893361-47-8 **$17.95**
For ages 7 & up

Spiritual Biographies for Young People—For ages 7 and up

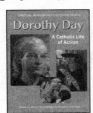
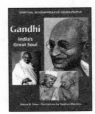
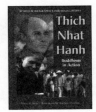

Black Elk: Native American Man of Spirit
by Maura D. Shaw; Full-color illus. by Stephen Marchesi
Through historically accurate illustrations and photos, inspiring age-appropriate activities and Black Elk's own words, this colorful biography introduces children to a remarkable person who ensured that the traditions and beliefs of his people would not be forgotten.
6¾ x 8¾, 32 pp, HC, Full-color and b/w illus., 978-1-59473-043-6 **$12.99**

Dorothy Day: A Catholic Life of Action
by Maura D. Shaw; Full-color illus. by Stephen Marchesi
Introduces children to one of the most inspiring women of the twentieth century, a down-to-earth spiritual leader who saw the presence of God in every person she met. Includes practical activities, a timeline and a list of important words to know.
6¾ x 8¾, 32 pp, HC, Full-color illus., 978-1-59473-011-5 **$12.99**

Gandhi: India's Great Soul
by Maura D. Shaw; Full-color illus. by Stephen Marchesi
There are a number of biographies of Gandhi written for young readers, but this is the only one that balances a simple text with illustrations, photographs, and activities that encourage children and adults to talk about how to make changes happen without violence. Introduces children to important concepts of freedom, equality and justice among people of all backgrounds and religions.
6¾ x 8¾, 32 pp, HC, Full-color illus., 978-1-893361-91-1 **$12.95**

Thich Nhat Hanh: Buddhism in Action
by Maura D. Shaw; Full-color illus. by Stephen Marchesi
Warm illustrations, photos, age-appropriate activities and Thich Nhat Hanh's own poems introduce a great man to children in a way they can understand and enjoy. Includes a list of important Buddhist words to know.
6¾ x 8¾, 32 pp, HC, Full-color illus., 978-1-893361-87-4 **$12.95**

Sacred Texts—SkyLight Illuminations Series

Offers today's spiritual seeker an accessible entry into the great classic texts of the world's spiritual traditions. Each classic is presented in an accessible translation, with facing pages of guided commentary from experts, giving you the keys you need to understand the history, context and meaning of the text. This series enables you, whatever your background, to experience and understand classic spiritual texts directly, and to make them a part of your life.

CHRISTIANITY

The End of Days: Essential Selections from Apocalyptic Texts—
Annotated & Explained *Annotation by Robert G. Clouse*
Helps you understand the complex Christian visions of the end of the world.
5½ x 8½, 224 pp, Quality PB, 978-1-59473-170-9 **$16.99**

The Hidden Gospel of Matthew: Annotated & Explained
Translation & Annotation by Ron Miller
Takes you deep into the text cherished around the world to discover the words and events that have the strongest connection to the historical Jesus.
5½ x 8½, 272 pp, Quality PB, 978-1-59473-038-2 **$16.99**

The Infancy Gospels of Jesus: Apocryphal Tales from the Childhoods of Mary and Jesus—Annotated & Explained *Stevan Davies; Foreword by A. Edward Siecienski*
A startling presentation of the early lives of Mary, Jesus, and other biblical figures that will amuse and surprise you. 5½ x 8½, 176 pp, Quality PB Original, 978-1-59473-258-4 **$16.99**

The Lost Sayings of Jesus: Teachings from Ancient Christian, Jewish, Gnostic and Islamic Sources—Annotated & Explained
Translation & Annotation by Andrew Phillip Smith; Foreword by Stephan A. Hoeller
This collection of more than three hundred sayings depicts Jesus as a Wisdom teacher who speaks to people of all faiths as a mystic and spiritual master.
5½ x 8½, 240 pp, Quality PB, 978-1-59473-172-3 **$16.99**

Philokalia: The Eastern Christian Spiritual Texts—Selections Annotated & Explained *Annotation by Allyne Smith; Translation by G. E. H. Palmer, Phillip Sherrard and Bishop Kallistos Ware*
The first approachable introduction to the wisdom of the Philokalia, which is the classic text of Eastern Christian spirituality.
5½ x 8½, 240 pp, Quality PB, 978-1-59473-103-7 **$16.99**

The Sacred Writings of Paul: Selections Annotated & Explained
Translation & Annotation by Ron Miller
Explores the apostle Paul's core message of spiritual equality, freedom and joy.
5½ x 8½, 224 pp, Quality PB, 978-1-59473-213-3 **$16.99**

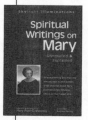

Sex Texts from the Bible: Selections Annotated & Explained
Translation & Annotation by Teresa J. Hornsby; Foreword by Amy-Jill Levine
Offers surprising insight into our modern sexual lives.
5½ x 8½, 208 pp, Quality PB, 978-1-59473-217-1 **$16.99**

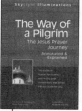

Spiritual Writings on Mary: Annotated & Explained
Annotation by Mary Ford-Grabowsky; Foreword by Andrew Harvey
Examines the role of Mary, the mother of Jesus, as a source of inspiration in history and in life today. 5½ x 8½, 288 pp, Quality PB, 978-1-59473-001-6 **$16.99**

The Way of a Pilgrim: The Jesus Prayer Journey—Annotated & Explained
Translation & Annotation by Gleb Pokrovsky; Foreword by Andrew Harvey
This classic of Russian spirituality is the delightful account of one man who sets out to learn the prayer of the heart, also known as the "Jesus prayer."
5½ x 8½, 160 pp, Illus., Quality PB, 978-1-893361-31-7 **$14.95**

Sacred Texts—cont.

MORMONISM

The Book of Mormon: Selections Annotated & Explained
Annotation by Jana Riess; Foreword by Phyllis Tickle
Explores the sacred epic that is cherished by more than twelve million members of the LDS church as the keystone of their faith.
5½ x 8½ , 272 pp, Quality PB, 978-1-59473-076-4 **$16.99**

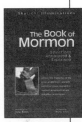

NATIVE AMERICAN

Native American Stories of the Sacred: Annotated & Explained
Retold & Annotated by Evan T. Pritchard
Intended for more than entertainment, these teaching tales contain elegantly simple illustrations of time-honored truths.
5½ x 8½, 272 pp, Quality PB, 978-1-59473-112-9 **$16.99**

GNOSTICISM

Gnostic Writings on the Soul: Annotated & Explained
Translation & Annotation by Andrew Phillip Smith; Foreword by Stephan A. Hoeller
Reveals the inspiring ways your soul can remember and return to its unique, divine purpose.
5½ x 8½, 144 pp, Quality PB, 978-1-59473-220-1 **$16.99**

The Gospel of Philip: Annotated & Explained
Translation & Annotation by Andrew Phillip Smith; Foreword by Stevan Davies
Reveals otherwise unrecorded sayings of Jesus and fragments of Gnostic mythology.
5½ x 8½, 160 pp, Quality PB, 978-1-59473-111-2 **$16.99**

The Gospel of Thomas: Annotated & Explained
Translation & Annotation by Stevan Davies Sheds new light on the origins of Christianity and portrays Jesus as a wisdom-loving sage.
5½ x 8½, 192 pp, Quality PB, 978-1-893361-45-4 **$16.99**

The Secret Book of John: The Gnostic Gospel—Annotated & Explained
Translation & Annotation by Stevan Davies The most significant and influential text of the ancient Gnostic religion.
5½ x 8½, 208 pp, Quality PB, 978-1-59473-082-5 **$16.99**

JUDAISM

The Divine Feminine in Biblical Wisdom Literature
Selections Annotated & Explained
Translation & Annotation by Rabbi Rami Shapiro; Foreword by Rev. Cynthia Bourgeault, PhD
Uses the Hebrew books of Psalms, Proverbs, Song of Songs, Ecclesiastes and Job, Wisdom literature and the Wisdom of Solomon to clarify who Wisdom is.
5½ x 8½, 240 pp, Quality PB, 978-1-59473-109-9 **$16.99**

Ethics of the Sages: *Pirke Avot*—Annotated & Explained
Translation & Annotation by Rabbi Rami Shapiro Clarifies the ethical teachings of the early Rabbis. 5½ x 8½, 192 pp, Quality PB, 978-1-59473-207-2 **$16.99**

Hasidic Tales: Annotated & Explained
Translation & Annotation by Rabbi Rami Shapiro
Introduces the legendary tales of the impassioned Hasidic rabbis, presenting them as stories rather than as parables. 5½ x 8½, 240 pp, Quality PB, 978-1-893361-86-7 **$16.95**

The Hebrew Prophets: Selections Annotated & Explained
Translation & Annotation by Rabbi Rami Shapiro; Foreword by Zalman M. Schachter-Shalomi
Focuses on the central themes covered by all the Hebrew prophets.
5½ x 8½, 224 pp, Quality PB, 978-1-59473-037-5 **$16.99**

Zohar: Annotated & Explained *Translation & Annotation by Daniel C. Matt*
The best-selling author of *The Essential Kabbalah* brings together in one place the most important teachings of the Zohar, the canonical text of Jewish mystical tradition.
5½ x 8½, 176 pp, Quality PB, 978-1-893361-51-5 **$15.99**

Sacred Texts—cont.

ISLAM

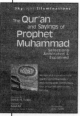

The Qur'an and Sayings of Prophet Muhammad
Selections Annotated & Explained
Annotation by Sohaib N. Sultan; Translation by Yusuf Ali; Revised by Sohaib N. Sultan
Foreword by Jane I. Smith
Explores how the timeless wisdom of the Qur'an can enrich your own spiritual
journey.
5½ x 8½, 256 pp, Quality PB, 978-1-59473-222-5 **$16.99**

Rumi and Islam: Selections from His Stories, Poems, and Discourses—
Annotated & Explained
Translation & Annotation by Ibrahim Gamard
Focuses on Rumi's place within the Sufi tradition of Islam, providing insight into
the mystical side of the religion.
5½ x 8½, 240 pp, Quality PB, 978-1-59473-002-3 **$15.99**

EASTERN RELIGIONS

The Art of War—Spirituality for Conflict
Annotated & Explained
*by Sun Tzu; Annotation by Thomas Huynh; Translation by Thomas Huynh and the Editors at
Sonshi.com; Foreword by Marc Benioff; Preface by Thomas Cleary*
Highlights principles that encourage a perceptive and spiritual approach to conflict.
5½ x 8½, 256 pp, Quality PB, 978-1-59473-244-7 **$16.99**

Bhagavad Gita: Annotated & Explained
Translation by Shri Purohit Swami; Annotation by Kendra Crossen Burroughs
Explains references and philosophical terms, shares the interpretations of famous
spiritual leaders and scholars, and more.
5½ x 8½, 192 pp, Quality PB, 978-1-893361-28-7 **$16.95**

Dhammapada: Annotated & Explained
Translation by Max Müller and revised by Jack Maguire; Annotation by Jack Maguire
Contains all of Buddhism's key teachings.
5½ x 8½, 160 pp, b/w photos, Quality PB, 978-1-893361-42-3 **$14.95**

Selections from the Gospel of Sri Ramakrishna
Annotated & Explained
Translation by Swami Nikhilananda; Annotation by Kendra Crossen Burroughs
Introduces the fascinating world of the Indian mystic and the universal appeal of
his message.
5½ x 8½, 240 pp, b/w photos, Quality PB, 978-1-893361-46-1 **$16.95**

Tao Te Ching: Annotated & Explained
Translation & Annotation by Derek Lin; Foreword by Lama Surya Das
Introduces an Eastern classic in an accessible, poetic and completely original way.
5½ x 8½, 192 pp, Quality PB, 978-1-59473-204-1 **$16.99**

STOICISM

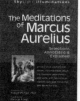

The Meditations of Marcus Aurelius
Selections Annotated & Explained
Annotation by Russell McNeil, PhD; Translation by George Long; Revised by Russell McNeil, PhD
Offers insightful and engaging commentary into the historical background of
Stoicism.
5½ x 8½, 288 pp, Quality PB, 978-1-59473-236-2 **$16.99**

Judaism / Christianity / Interfaith

Getting to the Heart of Interfaith: The Eye-Opening, Hope-Filled Friendship of a Pastor, a Rabbi and a Sheikh
by Pastor Don Mackenzie, Rabbi Ted Falcon and Sheikh Jamal Rahman
Offers many insights and encouragements for individuals and groups who want to tap into the promise of interfaith dialogue. 6 x 9, 192 pp, Quality PB, 978-1-59473-263-8 **$16.99**

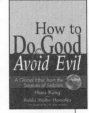

How to Do Good and Avoid Evil: A Global Ethic from the Sources of Judaism by *Hans Küng and Rabbi Walter Homolka; Translated by Rev. Dr. John Bowden*
Explores how the principles of a global ethic can be found in Judaism.
6 x 9, 224 pp, HC, 978-1-59473-255-3 **$19.99**

Hearing the Call across Traditions: Readings on Faith and Service
Edited by Adam Davis; Foreword by Eboo Patel Explores the connections between faith, service, and social justice through the prose, verse, and sacred texts of the world's great faith traditions. 6 x 9, 352 pp, HC, 978-1-59473-264-5 **$29.99**

The Jewish Approach to Repairing the World (Tikkun Olam)
A Brief Introduction for Christians *by Rabbi Elliot N. Dorff, PhD, with Reverend Cory Willson*
A window into the Jewish idea of responsibility to care for the world.
5½ x 8½, 256 pp, Quality PB, 978-1-58023-349-1 **$16.99** *(A book from Jewish Lights, SkyLight Paths' sister imprint)*

Modern Jews Engage the New Testament: Enhancing Jewish Well-Being in a Christian Environment *by Rabbi Michael J. Cook, PhD*
A look at the dynamics of the New Testament. 6 x 9, 416 pp, HC, 978-1-58023-313-2 **$29.99**
(A book from Jewish Lights, SkyLight Paths' sister imprint)

The Changing Christian World: A Brief Introduction for Jews
by Rabbi Leonard A. Schoolman 5½ x 8½, 176 pp, Quality PB, 978-1-58023-344-6 **$16.99**
(A book from Jewish Lights, SkyLight Paths' sister imprint)

Christians and Jews in Dialogue: Learning in the Presence of the Other
by Mary C. Boys and Sara S. Lee; Foreword by Dorothy C. Bass
6 x 9, 240 pp, HC, 978-1-59473-144-0 **$21.99**

Disaster Spiritual Care: Practical Clergy Responses to Community, Regional and National Tragedy *Edited by Rabbi Stephen B. Roberts, BCJC, & Rev. Willard W.C. Ashley, Sr., DMin, DH*
6 x 9, 384 pp, HC, 978-1-59473-240-9 **$40.00**

Interactive Faith: The Essential Interreligious Community-Building Handbook
Edited by Rev. Bud Heckman 6 x 9, 304 pp, HC, 978-1-59473-237-9 **$40.00**

The Jewish Approach to God: A Brief Introduction for Christians *by Rabbi Neil Gillman*
5½ x 8½, 192 pp, Quality PB, 978-1-58023-190-9 **$16.95** *(A book from Jewish Lights, SkyLight Paths' sister imprint)*

The Jewish Connection to Israel, the Promised Land: A Brief Introduction for Christians *by Rabbi Eugene Korn, PhD* 5½ x 8½, 192 pp, Quality PB, 978-1-58023-318-7 **$14.99**
(A book from Jewish Lights, SkyLight Paths' sister imprint)

Jewish Holidays: A Brief Introduction for Christians *by Rabbi Kerry M. Olitzky and Rabbi Daniel Judson* 5½ x 8½, 176 pp, Quality PB, 978-1-58023-302-6 **$16.99**
(A book from Jewish Lights, SkyLight Paths' sister imprint)

Jewish Ritual: A Brief Introduction for Christians
by Rabbi Kerry M. Olitzky and Rabbi Daniel Judson 5½ x 8½, 144 pp, Quality PB, 978-1-58023-210-4 **$14.99**
(A book from Jewish Lights, SkyLight Paths' sister imprint)

Jewish Spirituality: A Brief Introduction for Christians *by Rabbi Lawrence Kushner*
5½ x 8½, 112 pp, Quality PB, 978-1-58023-150-3 **$12.95** *(A book from Jewish Lights, SkyLight Paths' sister imprint)*

A Jewish Understanding of the New Testament *by Rabbi Samuel Sandmel;*
new Preface by Rabbi David Sandmel* 5½ x 8½, 368 pp, Quality PB, 978-1-59473-048-1 **$19.99**

Talking about God: Exploring the Meaning of Religious Life with Kierkegaard, Buber, Tillich and Heschel *by Daniel F. Polish, PhD* 6 x 9, 176 pp, HC, 978-1-59473-230-0 **$21.99**

We Jews and Jesus: Exploring Theological Differences for Mutual Understanding
by Rabbi Samuel Sandmel; new Preface by Rabbi David Sandmel A Classic Reprint
6 x 9, 192 pp, Quality PB, 978-1-59473-208-9 **$16.99**

Midrash Fiction / Folktales

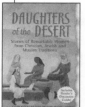

Abraham's Bind & Other Bible Tales of Trickery, Folly, Mercy and Love by Michael J. Caduto
New retellings of episodes in the lives of familiar biblical characters explore relevant life lessons.
6 x 9, 224 pp, HC, 978-1-59473-186-0 **$19.99**

Daughters of the Desert: Stories of Remarkable Women from Christian, Jewish and Muslim Traditions by Claire Rudolf Murphy, Meghan Nuttall Sayres, Mary Cronk Farrell, Sarah Conover and Betsy Wharton
Breathes new life into the old tales of our female ancestors in faith. Uses traditional scriptural passages as starting points, then with vivid detail fills in historical context and place. Chapters reveal the voices of Sarah, Hagar, Huldah, Esther, Salome, Mary Magdalene, Lydia, Khadija, Fatima and many more. Historical fiction ideal for readers of all ages. Quality paperback includes reader's discussion guide.
5½ x 8½, 192 pp, Quality PB, 978-1-59473-106-8 **$14.99**
HC, 192 pp, 978-1-893361-72-0 **$19.95**

The Triumph of Eve & Other Subversive Bible Tales
by Matt Biers-Ariel
Many people were taught and remember only a one-dimensional Bible. These engaging retellings are the antidote to this—they're witty, often hilarious, always profound, and invite you to grapple with questions and issues that are often hidden in the original text.
5½ x 8½, 192 pp, Quality PB, 978-1-59473-176-1 **$14.99**
Also avail.: **The Triumph of Eve Teacher's Guide**
8½ x 11, 44 pp, PB, 978-1-59473-152-5 **$8.99**

Wisdom in the Telling
Finding Inspiration and Grace in Traditional Folktales and Myths Retold
by Lorraine Hartin-Gelardi
6 x 9, 224 pp, HC, 978-1-59473-185-3 **$19.99**

Religious Etiquette / Reference

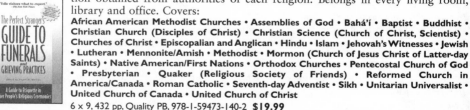

How to Be a Perfect Stranger, 4th Edition: The Essential Religious Etiquette Handbook Edited by Stuart M. Matlins and Arthur J. Magida
The indispensable guidebook to help the well-meaning guest when visiting other people's religious ceremonies. A straightforward guide to the rituals and celebrations of the major religions and denominations in the United States and Canada from the perspective of an interested guest of any other faith, based on information obtained from authorities of each religion. Belongs in every living room, library and office. Covers:
African American Methodist Churches • Assemblies of God • Bahá'í • Baptist • Buddhist • Christian Church (Disciples of Christ) • Christian Science (Church of Christ, Scientist) • Churches of Christ • Episcopalian and Anglican • Hindu • Islam • Jehovah's Witnesses • Jewish • Lutheran • Mennonite/Amish • Methodist • Mormon (Church of Jesus Christ of Latter-day Saints) • Native American/First Nations • Orthodox Churches • Pentecostal Church of God • Presbyterian • Quaker (Religious Society of Friends) • Reformed Church in America/Canada • Roman Catholic • Seventh-day Adventist • Sikh • Unitarian Universalist • United Church of Canada • United Church of Christ
6 x 9, 432 pp, Quality PB, 978-1-59473-140-2 **$19.99**

The Perfect Stranger's Guide to Funerals and Grieving Practices: A Guide to Etiquette in Other People's Religious Ceremonies Edited by Stuart M. Matlins
6 x 9, 240 pp, Quality PB, 978-1-893361-20-1 **$16.95**

The Perfect Stranger's Guide to Wedding Ceremonies: A Guide to Etiquette in Other People's Religious Ceremonies Edited by Stuart M. Matlins
6 x 9, 208 pp, Quality PB, 978-1-893361-19-5 **$16.95**

Spiritual Biography / Reference

Hearing the Call across Traditions
Readings on Faith and Service
Edited by Adam Davis; Foreword by Eboo Patel
Explores the connections between faith, service, and social justice through the prose, verse, and sacred texts of the world's great faith traditions.
6 x 9, 352 pp, HC, 978-1-59473-264-5 **$29.99**

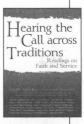

Spiritual Leaders Who Changed the World
The Essential Handbook to the Past Century of Religion
Edited by Ira Rifkin and the Editors at SkyLight Paths; Foreword by Dr. Robert Coles
An invaluable reference to the most important spiritual leaders of the past 100 years.
6 x 9, 304 pp, 15+ b/w photos, Quality PB, 978-1-59473-241-6 **$18.99**

Spiritual Biography—SkyLight Lives

SkyLight Lives reintroduces the lives and works of key spiritual figures of our time—people who by their teaching or example have challenged our assumptions about spirituality and have caused us to look at it in new ways.

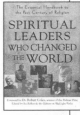

The Life of Evelyn Underhill
An Intimate Portrait of the Groundbreaking Author of Mysticism
by Margaret Cropper; Foreword by Dana Greene
Evelyn Underhill was a passionate writer and teacher who wrote elegantly on mysticism, worship, and devotional life.
6 x 9, 288 pp, 5 b/w photos, Quality PB, 978-1-893361-70-6 **$18.95**

Mahatma Gandhi: His Life and Ideas
by Charles F. Andrews; Foreword by Dr. Arun Gandhi
Examines from a contemporary Christian activist's point of view the religious ideas and political dynamics that influenced the birth of the peaceful resistance movement.
6 x 9, 336 pp, 5 b/w photos, Quality PB, 978-1-893361-89-8 **$18.95**

Simone Weil: A Modern Pilgrimage
by Robert Coles
The extraordinary life of the spiritual philosopher who's been called both saint and madwoman.
6 x 9, 208 pp, Quality PB, 978-1-893361-34-8 **$16.95**

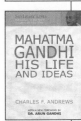

Zen Effects: The Life of Alan Watts
by Monica Furlong
Through his widely popular books and lectures, Alan Watts (1915–1973) did more to introduce Eastern philosophy and religion to Western minds than any figure before or since.
6 x 9, 264 pp, Quality PB, 978-1-893361-32-4 **$16.95**

More Spiritual Biography

Bede Griffiths: An Introduction to His Interspiritual Thought
by Wayne Teasdale
The first study of his contemplative experience and thought, exploring the intersection of Hinduism and Christianity.
6 x 9, 288 pp, Quality PB, 978-1-893361-77-5 **$18.95**

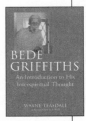

The Soul of the Story: Meetings with Remarkable People
by Rabbi David Zeller
Inspiring and entertaining, this compelling collection of spiritual adventures assures us that no spiritual lesson truly learned is ever lost.
6 x 9, 288 pp, HC, 978-1-58023-272-2 **$21.99**
(A book from Jewish Lights, SkyLight Paths' sister imprint)

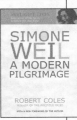

Spiritual Poetry—The Mystic Poets

Experience these mystic poets as you never have before. Each beautiful, compact book includes: a brief introduction to the poet's time and place; a summary of the major themes of the poet's mysticism and religious tradition; essential selections from the poet's most important works; and an appreciative preface by a contemporary spiritual writer.

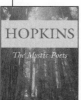

Hafiz
The Mystic Poets
Preface by Ibrahim Gamard
Hafiz is known throughout the world as Persia's greatest poet, with sales of his poems in Iran today only surpassed by those of the Qur'an itself. His probing and joyful verse speaks to people from all backgrounds who long to taste and feel divine love and experience harmony with all living things.
5 x 7¼, 144 pp, HC, 978-1-59473-009-2 **$16.99**

Hopkins
The Mystic Poets
Preface by Rev. Thomas Ryan, CSP
Gerard Manley Hopkins, Christian mystical poet, is beloved for his use of fresh language and startling metaphors to describe the world around him. Although his verse is lovely, beneath the surface lies a searching soul, wrestling with and yearning for God.
5 x 7¼, 112 pp, HC, 978-1-59473-010-8 **$16.99**

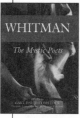

Tagore
The Mystic Poets
Preface by Swami Adiswarananda
Rabindranath Tagore is often considered the "Shakespeare" of modern India. A great mystic, Tagore was the teacher of W. B. Yeats and Robert Frost, the close friend of Albert Einstein and Mahatma Gandhi, and the winner of the Nobel Prize for Literature. This beautiful sampling of Tagore's two most important works, *The Gardener* and *Gitanjali*, offers a glimpse into his spiritual vision that has inspired people around the world.
5 x 7¼, 144 pp, HC, 978-1-59473-008-5 **$16.99**

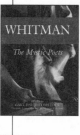

Whitman
The Mystic Poets
Preface by Gary David Comstock
Walt Whitman was the most innovative and influential poet of the nineteenth century. This beautiful sampling of Whitman's most important poetry from *Leaves of Grass,* and selections from his prose writings, offers a glimpse into the spiritual side of his most radical themes—love for country, love for others, and love of Self.
5 x 7¼, 192 pp, HC, 978-1-59473-041-2 **$16.99**

Journeys of Simplicity
Traveling Light with Thomas Merton, Bashō, Edward Abbey, Annie Dillard & Others
Invites you to consider a more graceful way of traveling through life. Use the included journal pages (in PB only) to help you get started on your own spiritual journey.

by Philip Harnden
5 x 7¼, 144 pp, Quality PB, 978-1-59473-181-5 **$12.99**
128 pp, HC, 978-1-893361-76-8 **$16.95**

Spirituality & Crafts

Beading—The Creative Spirit: Finding Your Sacred Center through the Art of Beadwork *by Rev. Wendy Ellsworth*
Invites you on a spiritual pilgrimage into the kaleidoscope world of glass and color.   7 x 9, 240 pp, 8-page full-color insert, plus b/w photographs and diagrams
Quality PB, 978-1-59473-267-6 **$18.99**

Contemplative Crochet: A Hands-On Guide for Interlocking Faith and Craft *by Cindy Crandall-Frazier; Foreword by Linda Skolnik*
Illuminates the spiritual lessons you can learn through crocheting.
7 x 9, 208 pp, b/w photographs, Quality PB, 978-1-59473-238-6 **$16.99**

The Knitting Way: A Guide to Spiritual Self-Discovery
by Linda Skolnik and Janice MacDaniels Examines how you can explore and strengthen your spiritual life through knitting.   7 x 9, 240 pp, b/w photographs
Quality PB, 978-1-59473-079-5 **$16.99**

The Painting Path: Embodying Spiritual Discovery through Yoga, Brush and Color *by Linda Novick; Foreword by Richard Segalman*
Explores the divine connection you can experience through creativity.
7 x 9, 208 pp, 8-page full-color insert, plus b/w photographs
Quality PB, 978-1-59473-226-3 **$18.99**

The Quilting Path: A Guide to Spiritual Discovery through Fabric, Thread and Kabbalah *by Louise Silk*
Explores how to cultivate personal growth through quilt making.
7 x 9, 192 pp, b/w photographs and illustrations, Quality PB, 978-1-59473-206-5 **$16.99**

The Scrapbooking Journey: A Hands-On Guide to Spiritual Discovery
by Cory Richardson-Lauve; Foreword by Stacy Julian Reveals how this craft can become a practice used to deepen and shape your life.
7 x 9, 176 pp, 8-page full-color insert, plus b/w photographs, Quality PB, 978-1-59473-216-4 **$18.99**

The Soulwork of Clay: A Hands-On Approach to Spirituality
by Marjory Zoet Bankson; Photographs by Peter Bankson
Takes you through the seven-step process of making clay into a pot, drawing parallels at each stage to the process of spiritual growth.
7 x 9, 192 pp, b/w photographs, Quality PB, 978-1-59473-249-2 **$16.99**

Kabbalah / Enneagram
(Books from Jewish Lights Publishing, SkyLight Paths' sister imprint)

God in Your Body: Kabbalah, Mindfulness and Embodied Spiritual Practice
by Jay Michaelson 6 x 9, 288 pp, Quality PB Original, 978-1-58023-304-0 **$18.99**

Cast in God's Image: Discover Your Personality Type Using the Enneagram and Kabbalah
by Rabbi Howard A. Addison 7 x 9, 176 pp, Quality PB, 978-1-58023-124-4 **$16.95**

Ehyeh: A Kabbalah for Tomorrow *by Dr. Arthur Green*
6 x 9, 224 pp, Quality PB, 978-1-58023-213-5 **$16.99**

The Enneagram and Kabbalah, 2nd Edition: Reading Your Soul
by Rabbi Howard A. Addison 6 x 9, 192 pp, Quality PB, 978-1-58023-229-6 **$16.99**

The Gift of Kabbalah: Discovering the Secrets of Heaven, Renewing Your Life on Earth
by Tamar Frankiel, PhD 6 x 9, 256 pp, Quality PB, 978-1-58023-141-1 **$16.95**
HC, 978-1-58023-108-4 **$21.95**

Kabbalah: A Brief Introduction for Christians
by Tamar Frankiel, PhD 5½ x 8½, 176 pp, Quality PB, 978-1-58023-303-3 **$16.99**

Zohar: Annotated & Explained *Translation and Annotation by Dr. Daniel C. Matt*
Foreword by Andrew Harvey 5½ x 8½, 176 pp, Quality PB, 978-1-893361-51-5 **$15.99**
(A book from Jewish Lights, SkyLight Paths' sister imprint)

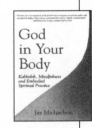

Spirituality of the Seasons

Autumn: A Spiritual Biography of the Season
Edited by Gary Schmidt and Susan M. Felch; Illustrations by Mary Azarian
Rejoice in autumn as a time of preparation and reflection. Includes Wendell Berry, David James Duncan, Robert Frost, A. Bartlett Giamatti, E. B. White, P. D. James, Julian of Norwich, Garret Keizer, Tracy Kidder, Anne Lamott, May Sarton.
6 x 9, 320 pp, 5 b/w illus., Quality PB, 978-1-59473-118-1 **$18.99**

Spring: A Spiritual Biography of the Season
Edited by Gary Schmidt and Susan M. Felch; Illustrations by Mary Azarian
Explore the gentle unfurling of spring and reflect on how nature celebrates rebirth and renewal. Includes Jane Kenyon, Lucy Larcom, Harry Thurston, Nathaniel Hawthorne, Noel Perrin, Annie Dillard, Martha Ballard, Barbara Kingsolver, Dorothy Wordsworth, Donald Hall, David Brill, Lionel Basney, Isak Dinesen, Paul Laurence Dunbar. 6 x 9, 352 pp, 6 b/w illus., Quality PB, 978-1-59473-246-1 **$18.99**

Summer: A Spiritual Biography of the Season
Edited by Gary Schmidt and Susan M. Felch; Illustrations by Barry Moser
"A sumptuous banquet.... These selections lift up an exquisite wholeness found within an everyday sophistication."— ★ *Publishers Weekly* starred review
Includes Anne Lamott, Luci Shaw, Ray Bradbury, Richard Selzer, Thomas Lynch, Walt Whitman, Carl Sandburg, Sherman Alexie, Madeleine L'Engle, Jamaica Kincaid.
6 x 9, 304 pp, 5 b/w illus., Quality PB, 978-1-59473-183-9 **$18.99**
HC, 978-1-59473-083-2 **$21.99**

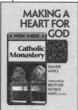

Winter: A Spiritual Biography of the Season
Edited by Gary Schmidt and Susan M. Felch; Illustrations by Barry Moser
"This outstanding anthology features top-flight nature and spirituality writers on the fierce, inexorable season of winter.... Remarkably lively and warm, despite the icy subject." — ★ *Publishers Weekly* starred review
Includes Will Campbell, Rachel Carson, Annie Dillard, Donald Hall, Ron Hansen, Jane Kenyon, Jamaica Kincaid, Barry Lopez, Kathleen Norris, John Updike, E. B. White.
6 x 9, 288 pp, 6 b/w illus., Deluxe PB w/flaps, 978-1-893361-92-8 **$18.95**

Spirituality / Animal Companions

Blessing the Animals: Prayers and Ceremonies to Celebrate God's Creatures, Wild and Tame *Edited by Lynn L. Caruso*
5¼ x 7¼, 256 pp, Quality PB, 978-1-59473-253-9 **$15.99**; HC, 978-1-59473-145-7 **$19.99**

Remembering My Pet: A Kid's Own Spiritual Workbook for When a Pet Dies
by Nechama Liss-Levinson, PhD, and Rev. Molly Phinney Baskette, MDiv; Foreword by Lynn L. Caruso
8 x 10, 48 pp, 2-color text, HC, 978-1-59473-221-3 **$16.99**

What Animals Can Teach Us about Spirituality: Inspiring Lessons from Wild and Tame Creatures *by Diana L. Guerrero* 6 x 9, 176 pp, Quality PB, 978-1-893361-84-3 **$16.95**

Spirituality—A Week Inside

Come and Sit: A Week Inside Meditation Centers
by Marcia Z. Nelson; Foreword by Wayne Teasdale
6 x 9, 224 pp, b/w photos, Quality PB, 978-1-893361-35-5 **$16.95**

Lighting the Lamp of Wisdom: A Week Inside a Yoga Ashram
by John Ittner; Foreword by Dr. David Frawley
6 x 9, 192 pp, 10+ b/w photos, Quality PB, 978-1-893361-52-2 **$15.95**

Making a Heart for God: A Week Inside a Catholic Monastery
by Dianne Aprile; Foreword by Brother Patrick Hart, OCSO
6 x 9, 224 pp, b/w photos, Quality PB, 978-1-893361-49-2 **$16.95**

Waking Up: A Week Inside a Zen Monastery
by Jack Maguire; Foreword by John Daido Loori, Roshi
6 x 9, 224 pp, b/w photos, Quality PB, 978-1-893361-55-3 **$16.95**; HC, 978-1-893361-13-3 **$21.95**

Spiritual Practice

Haiku—The Sacred Art: A Spiritual Practice in Three Lines
by Margaret D. McGee Introduces haiku as a simple and effective way of tapping into the sacred moments that permeate everyday living.
5½ x 8½, 192 pp, Quality PB, 978-1-59473-269-0 **$16.99**

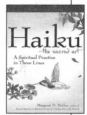

Dance—The Sacred Art: The Joy of Movement as a Spiritual Practice
by Cynthia Winton-Henry Invites all of us, regardless of experience, into the possibility of dance/movement as a spiritual practice.
5½ x 8½, 224 pp, Quality PB, 978-1-59473-268-3 **$16.99**

Spiritual Adventures in the Snow: Skiing & Snowboarding as Renewal for Your Soul *by Dr. Marcia McFee and Rev. Karen Foster; Foreword by Paul Arthur* Explores snow sports as tangible experiences of the spiritual essence of our bodies and the earth. 5½ x 8½, 208 pp, Quality PB, 978-1-59473-270-6 **$16.99**

Recovery—The Sacred Art: The Twelve Steps as Spiritual Practice
by Rami Shapiro; Foreword by Joan Borysenko, PhD Uniquely interprets the Twelve Steps of Alcoholics Anonymous to speak to everyone seeking a freer and more God-centered life. 5½ x 8½, 240 pp, Quality PB, 978-1-59473-259-1 **$16.99**

Soul Fire: Accessing Your Creativity *by Rev. Thomas Ryan, CSP*
Shows you how to cultivate your creative spirit as a way to encourage personal growth.
6 x 9, 160 pp, Quality PB, 978-1-59473-243-8 **$16.99**

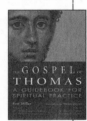

Running—The Sacred Art: Preparing to Practice
by Dr. Warren A. Kay; Foreword by Kristin Armstrong Examines how your daily run can enrich your spiritual life. 5½ x 8½, 160 pp, Quality PB, 978-1-59473-227-0 **$16.99**

Everyday Herbs in Spiritual Life: A Guide to Many Practices
by Michael J. Caduto; Foreword by Rosemary Gladstar
7 x 9, 208 pp, 21 b/w illustrations, Quality PB, 978-1-59473-174-7 **$16.99**

Divining the Body: Reclaim the Holiness of Your Physical Self *by Jan Phillips*
8 x 8, 256 pp, Quality PB, 978-1-59473-080-1 **$16.99**

The Gospel of Thomas: A Guidebook for Spiritual Practice
by Ron Miller; Translations by Stevan Davies 6 x 9, 160 pp, Quality PB, 978-1-59473-047-4 **$14.99**

Hospitality—The Sacred Art: Discovering the Hidden Spiritual Power of Invitation and Welcome *by Rev. Nanette Sawyer; Foreword by Rev. Dirk Ficca*
5½ x 8½, 192 pp, Quality PB, 978-1-59473-228-7 **$16.99**

Labyrinths from the Outside In: Walking to Spiritual Insight—A Beginner's Guide
by Donna Schaper and Carole Ann Camp
6 x 9, 208 pp, b/w illus. and photos, Quality PB, 978-1-893361-18-8 **$16.95**

Practicing the Sacred Art of Listening: A Guide to Enrich Your Relationships and Kindle Your Spiritual Life *by Kay Lindahl* 8 x 8, 176 pp, Quality PB, 978-1-893361-85-0 **$16.95**

The Sacred Art of Bowing: Preparing to Practice
by Andi Young 5½ x 8½, 128 pp, b/w illus., Quality PB, 978-1-893361-82-9 **$14.95**

The Sacred Art of Chant: Preparing to Practice
by Ana Hernández 5½ x 8½, 192 pp, Quality PB, 978-1-59473-036-8 **$15.99**

The Sacred Art of Fasting: Preparing to Practice
by Thomas Ryan, CSP 5½ x 8½, 192 pp, Quality PB, 978-1-59473-078-8 **$15.99**

The Sacred Art of Forgiveness: Forgiving Ourselves and Others through God's Grace
by Marcia Ford 8 x 8, 176 pp, Quality PB, 978-1-59473-175-4 **$16.99**

The Sacred Art of Listening: Forty Reflections for Cultivating a Spiritual Practice
by Kay Lindahl; Illustrations by Amy Schnapper
8 x 8, 160 pp, b/w illus., Quality PB, 978-1-893361-44-7 **$16.99**

The Sacred Art of Lovingkindness: Preparing to Practice
by Rabbi Rami Shapiro; Foreword by Marcia Ford 5½ x 8½, 176 pp, Quality PB, 978-1-59473-151-8 **$16.99**

Sacred Speech: A Practical Guide for Keeping Spirit in Your Speech
by Rev. Donna Schaper 6 x 9, 176 pp, Quality PB, 978-1-59473-068-9 **$15.99**
HC, 978-1-893361-74-4 **$21.95**

Thanking & Blessing—The Sacred Art: Spiritual Vitality through Gratefulness
by Jay Marshall, PhD; Foreword by Philip Gulley 5½ x 8½, 176 pp, Quality PB, 978-1-59473-231-7 **$16.99**

Spirituality

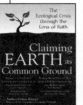

Claiming Earth as Common Ground: The Ecological Crisis through the Lens of Faith *by Andrea Cohen-Kiener; Foreword by Rev. Sally Bingham*
Inspires us to work across denominational lines in order to fulfill our sacred imperative to care for God's creation. 6 x 9, 192 pp, Quality PB, 978-1-59473-261-4 **$16.99**

The Losses of Our Lives: The Sacred Gifts of Renewal in Everyday Loss
by Dr. Nancy Copeland-Payton
Reframes loss from the perspective that our everyday losses help us learn what we need to handle the major losses. 6 x 9, 192 pp, HC, 978-1-59473-271-3 **$19.99**

The Workplace and Spirituality: New Perspectives on Research and Practice *Edited by Dr. Joan Marques, Dr. Satinder Dhiman and Dr. Richard King*
Explores the benefits of workplace spirituality in making work more meaningful and rewarding. 6 x 9, 256 pp, HC, 978-1-59473-260-7 **$29.99**

A Spirituality for Brokenness: Discovering Your Deepest Self in Difficult Times *by Terry Taylor*
Guides you through a compassionate yet highly practical process of facing, accepting, and finally integrating your brokenness into your life—a process that can ultimately bring mending. 6 x 9, 176 pp, Quality PB, 978-1-59473-229-4 **$16.99**

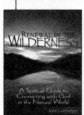

Next to Godliness: Finding the Sacred in Housekeeping
Edited and with Introductions by Alice Peck
Offers new perspectives on how we can reach out for the Divine.
6 x 9, 224 pp, Quality PB, 978-1-59473-214-0 **$19.99**

Bread, Body, Spirit: Finding the Sacred in Food
Edited and with Introductions by Alice Peck
Explores how food feeds our faith. 6 x 9, 224 pp, Quality PB, 978-1-59473-242-3 **$19.99**

Renewal in the Wilderness: A Spiritual Guide to Connecting with God in the Natural World *by John Lionberger*
Reveals the power of experiencing God's presence in many variations of the natural world. 6 x 9, 176 pp, b/w photos, Quality PB, 978-1-59473-219-5 **$16.99**

Honoring Motherhood: Prayers, Ceremonies and Blessings
Edited and with Introductions by Lynn L. Caruso
Journey through the seasons of motherhood. 5 x 7¼, 272 pp, HC, 978-1-59473-239-3 **$19.99**

Soul Fire: Accessing Your Creativity *by Rev. Thomas Ryan, CSP*
Learn to cultivate your creative spirit. 6 x 9, 160 pp, Quality PB, 978-1-59473-243-0 **$16.99**

Money and the Way of Wisdom: Insights from the Book of Proverbs
by Timothy J. Sandoval, PhD 6 x 9, 192 pp, Quality PB, 978-1-59473-245-4 **$16.99**

Creating a Spiritual Retirement: A Guide to the Unseen Possibilities in Our Lives
by Molly Srode 6 x 9, 208 pp, b/w photos, Quality PB, 978-1-59473-050-4 **$14.99**
HC, 978-1-893361-75-1 **$19.95**

Finding Hope: Cultivating God's Gift of a Hopeful Spirit
by Marcia Ford 8 x 8, 200 pp, Quality PB, 978-1-59473-211-9 **$16.99**

Jewish Spirituality: A Brief Introduction for Christians *by Lawrence Kushner*
5½ x 8½, 112 pp, Quality PB, 978-1-58023-150-3 **$12.95** *(A book from Jewish Lights, SkyLight Paths' sister imprint)*

Journeys of Simplicity: Traveling Light with Thomas Merton, Bashō, Edward Abbey, Annie Dillard & Others *by Philip Harnden*
5 x 7¼, 144 pp, Quality PB, 978-1-59473-181-5 **$12.99**; 128 pp, HC, 978-1-893361-76-8 **$16.95**

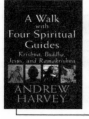

Keeping Spiritual Balance As We Grow Older: More than 65 Creative Ways to Use Purpose, Prayer, and the Power of Spirit to Build a Meaningful Retirement
by Molly and Bernie Srode 8 x 8, 224 pp, Quality PB, 978-1-59473-042-9 **$16.99**

Spiritually Incorrect: Finding God in All the Wrong Places *by Dan Wakefield; Illus. by Marian DelVecchio* 5½ x 8½, 192 pp, b/w illus., Quality PB, 978-1-59473-137-2 **$15.99**

A Walk with Four Spiritual Guides: Krishna, Buddha, Jesus, and Ramakrishna
by Andrew Harvey 5½ x 8½, 192 pp, 10 b/w photos & illus., Quality PB, 978-1-59473-138-9 **$15.99**

Prayer / Meditation

Sacred Attention: A Spiritual Practice for Finding God in the Moment
by Margaret D. McGee
Framed on the Christian liturgical year, this inspiring guide explores ways to develop a practice of attention as a means of talking—and listening—to God.
6 x 9, 144 pp, HC, 978-1-59473-232-4 **$19.99**

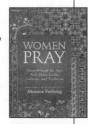

Women Pray: Voices through the Ages, from Many Faiths, Cultures and Traditions
Edited and with Introductions by Monica Furlong
5 x 7¼, 256 pp, Quality PB, 978-1-59473-071-9 **$15.99**

Women of Color Pray: Voices of Strength, Faith, Healing, Hope and Courage *Edited and with Introductions by Christal M. Jackson*
Through these prayers, poetry, lyrics, meditations and affirmations, you will share in the strong and undeniable connection women of color share with God.
5 x 7¼, 208 pp, Quality PB, 978-1-59473-077-1 **$15.99**

Secrets of Prayer: A Multifaith Guide to Creating Personal Prayer in Your Life *by Nancy Corcoran, CSJ*
This compelling, multifaith guidebook offers you companionship and encouragement on the journey to a healthy prayer life. 6 x 9, 160 pp, Quality PB, 978-1-59473-215-7 **$16.99**

Prayers to an Evolutionary God
by William Cleary; Afterword by Diarmuid O'Murchu
Inspired by the spiritual and scientific teachings of Diarmuid O'Murchu and Teilhard de Chardin, reveals that religion and science can be combined to create an expanding view of the universe—an evolutionary faith.
6 x 9, 208 pp, HC, 978-1-59473-006-1 **$21.99**

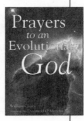

The Art of Public Prayer: Not for Clergy Only *by Lawrence A. Hoffman*
6 x 9, 288 pp, Quality PB, 978-1-893361-06-5 **$18.99**

A Heart of Stillness: A Complete Guide to Learning the Art of Meditation
by David A. Cooper 5½ x 8½, 272 pp, Quality PB, 978-1-893361-03-4 **$16.95**

Meditation without Gurus: A Guide to the Heart of Practice
by Clark Strand 5½ x 8½, 192 pp, Quality PB, 978-1-893361-93-5 **$16.95**

Praying with Our Hands: 21 Practices of Embodied Prayer from the World's Spiritual Traditions *by Jon M. Sweeney; Photographs by Jennifer J. Wilson; Foreword by Mother Tessa Bielecki; Afterword by Taitetsu Unno, PhD*
8 x 8, 96 pp, 22 duotone photos, Quality PB, 978-1-893361-16-4 **$16.95**

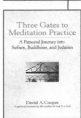

Silence, Simplicity & Solitude: A Complete Guide to Spiritual Retreat at Home
by David A. Cooper 5½ x 8½, 336 pp, Quality PB, 978-1-893361-04-1 **$16.95**

Three Gates to Meditation Practice: A Personal Journey into Sufism, Buddhism, and Judaism *by David A. Cooper* 5½ x 8½, 240 pp, Quality PB, 978-1-893361-22-5 **$16.95**

Prayer / M. Basil Pennington, OCSO

Finding Grace at the Center, 3rd Ed.: The Beginning of Centering Prayer *with Thomas Keating, OCSO, and Thomas E. Clarke, SJ; Foreword by Rev. Cynthia Bourgeault, PhD*
A practical guide to a simple and beautiful form of meditative prayer.
5 x 7¼, 128 pp, Quality PB, 978-1-59473-182-2 **$12.99**

The Monks of Mount Athos: A Western Monk's Extraordinary Spiritual Journey on Eastern Holy Ground *Foreword by Archimandrite Dionysios*
Explores the landscape, the monastic communities, and the food of Athos.
6 x 9, 256 pp, 10+ b/w drawings, Quality PB, 978-1-893361-78-2 **$18.95**

Psalms: A Spiritual Commentary *Illustrations by Phillip Ratner*
Reflections on some of the most beloved passages from the Bible's most widely read book. 6 x 9, 176 pp, 24 full-page b/w illus., Quality PB, 978-1-59473-234-8 **$16.99**
HC, 978-1-59473-141-9 **$19.99**

The Song of Songs: A Spiritual Commentary *Illustrations by Phillip Ratner*
Explore the Bible's most challenging mystical text.
6 x 9, 160 pp, 14 b/w illus., Quality PB, 978-1-59473-235-3 **$16.99**; HC, 978-1-59473-004-7 **$19.99**

AVAILABLE FROM BETTER BOOKSTORES.
TRY YOUR BOOKSTORE FIRST.

About SKYLIGHT PATHS Publishing

SkyLight Paths Publishing is creating a place where people of different spiritual traditions come together for challenge and inspiration, a place where we can help each other understand the mystery that lies at the heart of our existence.

Through spirituality, our religious beliefs are increasingly becoming a part of our lives—rather than *apart* from our lives. While many of us may be more interested than ever in spiritual growth, we may be less firmly planted in traditional religion. Yet, we do want to deepen our relationship to the sacred, to learn from our own as well as from other faith traditions, and to practice in new ways.

SkyLight Paths sees both believers and seekers as a community that increasingly transcends traditional boundaries of religion and denomination—people wanting to learn from each other, *walking together, finding the way.*

For your information and convenience, at the back of this book we have provided a list of other SkyLight Paths books you might find interesting and useful. They cover the following subjects:

Buddhism / Zen	Global Spiritual	Monasticism
Catholicism	Perspectives	Mysticism
Children's Books	Gnosticism	Poetry
Christianity	Hinduism /	Prayer
Comparative	Vedanta	Religious Etiquette
Religion	Inspiration	Retirement
Current Events	Islam / Sufism	Spiritual Biography
Earth-Based	Judaism	Spiritual Direction
Spirituality	Kabbalah	Spirituality
Enneagram	Meditation	Women's Interest
	Midrash Fiction	Worship

Or phone, fax, mail or e-mail to: SKYLIGHT PATHS Publishing
Sunset Farm Offices, Route 4 • P.O. Box 237 • Woodstock, Vermont 05091
Tel: (802) 457-4000 • Fax: (802) 457-4004 • www.skylightpaths.com
Credit card orders: (800) 962-4544 (8:30AM–5:30PM ET Monday–Friday)
Generous discounts on quantity orders. SATISFACTION GUARANTEED. Prices subject to change.

For more information about each book,
visit our website at www.skylightpaths.com